THE DECORATIVE ARTS OF SWEDEN

BY

IONA PLATH

DOVER PUBLICATIONS, INC., NEW YORK

Published in Canada by General Publishing Co.,
Ltd., 30 Lesmill Road, Don Mills, Toronto, On-
tario.
Published in the United Kingdom by Constable
and Co., Ltd., 10 Orange Street, London W.C.2.

This Dover edition, first published in 1966, is a
corrected republication of the work first published
by Charles Scribner's Sons in 1948. The text is
unabridged, but the Color Section of the original
publication has been omitted in the present edition.
An Index has been specially prepared for this
edition by the author.

Standard Book Number: 486-21478-8

Library of Congress Catalog Card Number: 65-20487

Manufactured in the United States of America

Dover Publications, Inc.
180 Varick Street
New York, N.Y. 10014

To My Husband
JAY ALAN

IN ACKNOWLEDGMENT

The research for this book was done in Stockholm, Sweden, at Nordiska Museum, Skansen Open-Air Museum, Svenska Slöjdföreningen, and the Hemslöjdsförbundet. I wish to take this opportunity to acknowledge my indebtedness to these great Swedish institutions, and to the Svenska Institutet För Kulturellt Utbyte Med Utlandet.

I am deeply grateful to Professor Fil. D:r Andreas Lindblom, Director of Nordiska and Skansen Museums, for graciously affording me every facility for study of the great collections of Swedish traditional forms at these museums.

I wish to thank Fil. dr Albert Eskeröd for his valuable assistance in planning my work in the peasantry section of Nordiska Museum.

I extend my thanks also to the following curators at Nordiska Museum:

Fil. lic. Gösta von Schoultz for his valuable, concrete assistance in the selection of examples of traditional wood, metal, and ceramics.

Fil. dr Anna-Maja Nylén for her generous help with traditional wooden utensils and peasantry articles of personal adornment, and for her sympathetic understanding of the requirements of my project.

Amanuens Elisabeth Strömberg for her assistance in the selection of Sweden's unique wall paintings and traditional textiles.

Special acknowledgment is due Sven-Erik Skawonius, Director of Svenska Slöjdföreningen, for his valued assistance in the selection of the modern material.

My thanks are due also to Arthur Hald, of *Form* Magazine, and to Elisa Hald-Steenberg for her assistance in collecting the modern material.

I am deeply appreciative of the co-operation of the contemporary designers of Sweden who made their work available for this book.

I should like to take this opportunity to thank my many other Swedish friends for their kindness and encouragement.

I want also to thank Charles Scribner's Sons, Wallace Meyer, of the staff of editors, and Atkinson Dymock, Art Director, for helping me to shape my presentation to this country of Sweden's decorative arts.

IONA PLATH

CONTENTS

LAPPLAND

NORRBOTTEN

VÄSTERBOTTEN

JÄMTLAND

ÅNGERMANLAND

Mattmar • • Kyrkås

MEDELPAD

HÄRJEDALEN   HÄLSINGLAND

Delsbo •
Järvsö •

Arbrå •

DALARNA

Mora • Siljan   • Gävle
Lima • Rättvik
Leksand   GÄST-
• Malung   RIKLAND

UPPLAND

Västerfärnebo •   • Uppsala
Flackebo •   Bred •
Lake Mälar   Norrby
VÄSTMANLAND   • Stockholm
Birka   Gustavsberg

VÄRMLAND

• Mellösa

NÄRKE   SÖDERMAN-
Ekeby •   LAND

DALSLAND   ÖSTER-
• Tängelanda   GÖTLAND
Odensåker   Vadstena •
Rogslösa •

BOHUSLÄN   Lidköping   Ukna •
Kasimirsborg •

VÄSTERGÖTLAND   GOTLAND

Göteborg •   Jönköping •

• Limmared   • Vetlanda

SMÅLAND
Orrefors •
Varberg •   Kosta •
Hovmantorp •   • Kalmar
HALLAND   Emmaboda •   ÖLAND

• Halmstad   • Knäred

BLEKINGE

Långaröd •

SKÅNE

0 ————————— 100
STATUTE MILES

A MAP OF SWEDEN

showing the provinces and some cities
and towns mentioned in this book.

LIST OF ILLUSTRATIONS

LIST OF ILLUSTRATIONS

LIST OF ILLUSTRATIONS

LIST OF ILLUSTRATIONS

LIST OF ILLUSTRATIONS

LIST OF ILLUSTRATIONS

LIST OF ILLUSTRATIONS

LIST OF ILLUSTRATIONS

LIST OF ILLUSTRATIONS

WALL PAINTINGS: DALARNA AND NORTHERN PROVINCES

xxiii

THE
DECORATIVE
ARTS OF SWEDEN

CHAPTER I

SWEDEN
PAST AND PRESENT

THE decorative arts of Sweden are evidence of the high esteem in which the Swedish people hold the home and everything pertaining to the home.

Sweden's geographical position undoubtedly has made its contribution to this deep-seated appreciation of the decorative arts as applied to the home, especially in former times. The winters in Sweden are long, dark, and cold; little work can be done out of doors, and rural families have always been obliged to spend the winter months largely within their homes. It was natural that the home and objects for the home should receive much attention and care.

During these dark months no member of the Swedish peasant family was allowed to be idle. While the women of the family worked their looms the men whittled and carved useful implements of wood. In the old days everything the family needed was made by some member at home. The products desired and required by royalty, by the clergy and by the burghers naturally fell into a different category. But, as in all countries, the objects associated with the peasantry are the most distinctive and therefore the most interesting from a decorative standpoint. The forms of the products, and the designs used to decorate them, show the extent to which the Swedish peasant clung to Scandinavian traditionary patterns.

The population of Sweden is remarkably homogeneous. Only in the extreme northern part are there people of "foreign" extraction, the Laplanders. Nomads of an old Arctic race, they live a wan-

dering life in and about the mountains of the far northwestern part of Sweden, and they speak a language of their own.

Along the eastern coast the peasant population is for the most part of Finnish descent. During the 16th and 17th centuries Finnish immigrants colonized sections of lower Sweden, having come to work in the great forest districts. They retained their own language and culture, which their descendants preserved, and even as late as the latter part of the 19th century traces of this colonization were distinguishable.

It might be assumed that in such a purely Scandinavian population the arts and crafts would have markedly typical characteristics. But Sweden is a country of widely diverging geographical conditions. In the very southern part the soil is rich and fertile, the climate similar to that of central Europe. In the central part the winters increase in length and in intensity of cold. In the northern part the land is barren and mountainous, reaching finally to the snowy wastes of the Arctic Circle. The conditions of existence in the various sections of Sweden naturally call for varying manners of living, habits, and work, which in turn result in a difference in home furnishings. There is a strong sectional divergence not only in form but in the ornamentation of the home furnishings. In the old days it was difficult to travel about the country, and during the short summer months when travel was at all feasible, the peasants, being part- or full-time farmers, had much work to do. Consequently there was little exchange of ideas and patterns among the

1

provinces, until this in itself became a tradition, with peasants clinging to old family design forms and those of the province in which they lived.

The differences were so marked that today those familiar with the peasant culture of the old times are able to identify objects as coming from certain provinces. And indeed, Swedish peasant art forms cannot be regarded as typical of Sweden so much as they are typical of the individual province from which they originated. Of course some outside influences crept in. Traveling merchants wandered about the summer countryside peddling their wares; many waterways with small boats carried other articles. These the peasants would purchase and use; but they were not prone to copy or imitate the new and unfamiliar style forms. When they did accept a form, however, they incorporated it into their own style.

In addition to the effect of the geographical and climatic conditions on style and form of the decorative arts, there was to some extent a foreign influence. Before the age of industry and commerce and the resulting international habits, this foreign influence was especially felt in the coastal provinces of southern Sweden — Skåne, Blekinge, and the Baltic Islands, Oland and Gotland. Taken as a whole, these provinces show essential differences from the culture of other Swedish peasantry, although they show also great differences within themselves. Sweden's grain comes from the fertile fields of Skåne, but because thick forests in the northern part separated it from adjacent parts of Sweden, Skåne's culture followed its own lines. When it did enter into connection with other countries the link was with Denmark and northern Germany. The people of Blekinge province were the seafaring people. Contact and trade with far distant places brought many style trends. Rococo designs from East Indian chinaware and flowers from silken textiles were motifs that were woven into colorful textiles along with their own traditional patterns. The skill with which these new motifs were adapted to the transposed legends and mysticism of the times gave the fabrics a richness that is characteristic of the province. Articles from the island of Gotland have a strong resemblance to those from Blekinge, while Oland's culture shows its relationship to that of countries west of Sweden.

To the north are the provinces of Småland, Halland, Bohuslän, and Dalsland, with a peasant culture more purely Swedish in character. Any foreign influence felt in the designs of these provinces was an indirect one resulting from trade with the more southern provinces.

In middle Sweden proper are the provinces of Västergötland, Ostergötland, Södermanland, Närke, Uppland. In these provinces, any faint trace of foreign influence gradually lessens, until in the most northern provinces it disappears completely.

The very heart of Swedish peasant culture is to be found in the next most northern provinces, those of Värmland, Västmanland and Dalarna. The statement holds especially of Dalarna. With impassable mountains and uncultivated lands to the west, the most ancient types of Swedish peasant culture were allowed to persist unchanged in Dalarna, flourishing to such an extent that any influence from the east left scarcely a trace.

The large remaining territory to the north is known as Norrland. Eight provinces make up this territory, which embraces almost two-thirds of the whole area of Sweden. The peasant home possessions of this large section show many differences, but the relationship between them is surprisingly strong. Apparently the reason lies in the fact that large rivers connect the cultivated tracts of coastal districts with the interior lake districts. Jämtland and Härjedalen border on Norway, and a Norwegian influence is perceptible in the form and decoration of objects in these provinces. An influence of the culture of the countries across the Baltic is seen in the home furnishings of the peasants living on the east coast. These two influences, merging with the more truly Swedish art forms in the interior of Norrland, produce that elasticity of form and that artistic richness which are especially characteristic of the culture of this comparatively extensive territory.

Swedish peasant culture was also influenced by that of the upper classes, made up of the nobility, the clergy, and the townspeople. The objects in use in these classes had strong international elements and reflected the style tendencies of successive periods on the Continent. Forms of culture other than those of the ancient Swedish peasant culture were making themselves felt as early as the Swedish Middle Ages, but with the Renaissance the effect of this culture of the higher classes became definitely stronger.

Peasant craftsmen could never equal the high skill and achieve the resulting graceful forms of the objects belonging to the higher classes, but certain details of decoration caught their fancy and were grafted on to their own folk styles, which finally settled down to a Swedish rural style. The Renaissance, which reached Sweden during the latter part of the 16th century, brought the vogue of low cupboards among the upper classes. The peasants imitated these cupboards after their own fashion, and their use survived up to the 18th century; in the peasant dwellings the low cupboards were placed in the corner of the room on benches fixed along the walls. Elaborate 16th-century tables had their effect also, inspiring the rural people to paint animals, wreaths and inscriptions on the tops of their own simply constructed tables.

Noticeable traits of British, Dutch-British, Italian and French modes are found in the furnishings belonging to the nobility of the Carolingian Period (1660-1720), so named from the successive Swedish kings Karl X, Karl XI, and Karl XII. During the 17th century the property of the higher classes was confiscated by Karl XI. An increase of importance for the middle classes ensued, and the Dutch-British style then began to gain dominance over the French. Faint traces of these style trends are to be seen in the peasant furniture of that time.

A period called "The Age of Fredrik I" (1720-1750) followed the great wars of Karl (or Charles) XII. An East India company was formed in Sweden for trade with China. Imported Chinese articles as well as imitations of such articles were favored by the upper classes, and again their effect is apparent in peasant embroideries of the southern provinces during that period.

In 1732, French craftsmen were brought to Stockholm to decorate the Royal Palace, and French rococo became dominant, as the English type of rococo had been. A typically Swedish rococo developed, building on Swedish traditions and characterized by rich coloring. The floral patterns caught the interest of the peasantry and were painted on their cupboards and chests.

By 1770 the Swedish rococo had been superseded by the Early Gustavian style (1770-1780), named after Gustav III. In this Swedish modification of the Louis XVI style, the clear, rich colors of the rococo gave way to pale pearl-grey tints, although some rococo still lingered in the wood carvings. By 1790-1810 the Late Gustavian style was well established, and symmetry and straight lines now offered a distinct contrast to the Early Gustavian splendor.

Changing taste was not alone responsible for this, as Sweden had passed many anti-luxury laws and ordinances. The new laws ruled out the use of woods and metals for sheer ornament, and the result was furniture that was more severe, with simple brass moldings. The Gustavian style became very popular and widespread, even in the rural districts, especially in northern Sweden. It flourished until 1825.

With the arrival of the newly elected Crown Prince Charles Jean (the French Marshal Bernadotte), the Empire style, derived from the Napoleonic Empire style, became popular. In Sweden it was known as the "Karl Johan" style (1810-1830). The mahogany furniture was again decorated with carvings and gilt wood was also used. Evidently the style held no inspiration for the peasants, as no traces are to be found in the peasant furnishings of that time.

By 1860, increasing industrialization introduced the modern type of furnishings. In a country where handicraft had been of great importance since ancient times, the advent of industrialism caused the arts and home crafts to stagnate. Only in the southern provinces had a complete livelihood from agriculture been possible. In the more northern parts climatic conditions had forced the peasants to eke out a living by other ways, and handicraft had been the answer. Thus, when industry forced out the need of hand-made articles, the rural population was obliged to move to factory areas, and instead of being self-sufficient producers they became factory workers.

The homes in the factory areas were small. There was no room for looms, and the women of the family could no longer carry on their traditional occupation. Consequently these peasants became the largest consumer class for the ready-made factory goods. In the first raw phases of industrialization there were no manufacturing traditions. Old patterns were simply copied in poor materials, with resulting poor finish and form. Taste quickly degenerated in all groups of society.

But this phase did not last long. Sweden foresaw the danger in the eventual effect on the people. Two great movements were initiated, one to protect home industry, and the other to improve the esthetic and technical quality of manufactured goods by stressing quality rather than quantity. The result was the international reputation for fine design which Sweden enjoys today.

Through the efforts of the *Svenska Hemslöjds-föreningarnas Riksförbund* (The National League of Swedish Home Craft Associations) and the *Svenska Hemslöjd* (Swedish Homecraft) Association, the old Swedish native arts have been revived. Realizing that the craftsmen would need a market for their products, the organizations provided one. Throughout Sweden are shops, systematically organized, which handle the homecraft products. Here one may see and purchase beautiful things of that indefinable charm that only handiwork joined to artistic endeavor can produce, and since the organizations strive to keep alive the special types of decoration of the various provinces, there is a great variety of articles.

The rural craftsmen are not required to leave their work in the shops on consignment. They are commissioned to do the work, and are furnished with patterns and color sketches made by Sweden's leading designers, who work with the *Hemslöjd** Association. These commissions are dealt out in awareness of the prevailing natural conditions of the various provinces. Exquisite hand-woven linen comes from those parts of Sweden where flax is grown. Simple, strong utility goods come from the more meagre sections; wooded areas supply the Association with beautiful and functional wooden articles and baskets; rich, colorful textiles come from the fertile plains in the South. The patterns are based on the traditional ones peculiar to each province. It is possible to purchase a fine copy of an old *rya* rug, a bit of *Flamsk* weaving, or lengths of double weave from the coastal districts. The shops not only cater to a retail trade but they in turn are commissioned by Sweden's large theaters, hotels, office buildings, stores, steamship and airway companies to supply them with fine linens, rugs, and wooden and hand-wrought iron articles.

This dual movement, which embraces the whole country, keeps alive a deep appreciation of technical skill and a feeling for style which has great cultural importance. Its economic importance is equally great, for many rural people now supplement their incomes and often derive their entire living from it. The resulting wealth of variety in

*Pronounced "Hemsloyd."

hand-loomed textiles and other homecrafts cannot be equaled in the whole world, and the fruits of the movement are evident everywhere in Sweden. Hand-loomed fabrics and rugs are not unusual in public buildings. For those who love beautiful things, Sweden is a most satisfying place.

The movement to improve industrial production has also given Sweden world acclaim for quality products of superior design. For this the *Svenska Slöjdföreningen* (Swedish Society of Arts and Crafts) is largely responsible. Founded as long ago as 1845, the Society has worked for the close collaboration of artists and industry, and objects of great artistic and technical merit have been the result. Another aim of the Society's program has been to raise the standard of home culture through exhibitions, lectures, study courses, and publications, an objective so successfully pursued that the movement has taken on a social character directed not toward limited groups but toward the entire people.

The Society has had a strong influence on style as well as on public taste. New types of low-priced home furnishings have been developed which are of excellent design. Designers are acclaimed on merit alone. People of all groups know the leaders in the various fields and appreciate their efforts. Encouragement is given to any young designer who is able to produce an article of artistic merit. It is not uncommon for a designer to repeat a special pattern every few years, bringing out, in effect, a new edition of an old motif. These are known and prized by the people; if the new version happens to be a hand-blocked fabric, one who cannot afford yardage will want to own at least enough for a wall hanging or a pillow top. Should such a person choose a gift of glass, a ceramic, or an article of pewter, his choice is determined by the design and the designer who fashioned it, for he knows his gift will be acceptable even if it is nothing more than a small ashtray.

Sweden is not only a rewarding country for people who love beautiful things, it is equally rewarding for those who endeavor to make beautiful things.

CHAPTER II

TEXTILES

To STUDY Swedish textiles is to study Sweden—history, customs, traditions, the people, and even the land itself, for all these enter into the patterns that have been woven into Swedish textiles as far back in past ages as records go.

Some fabrics have been preserved from the Swedish Middle Ages (1050-1500). These are of course very rare, and nothing can be said as to what was typical or common among the peasants at those early times. Form, decoration, and function of comparatively late peasant textiles indicate that at least some weaving methods and certain embroideries worked on counted threads have been practised with little alteration from as early as the Viking Age (800-1050). To trace the origin of some richly woven patterns it is necessary to go back as far as the Romanesque period (13th century). During the course of centuries these designs have become traditional.

A cushion, coverlet, or piece of fine linen, well woven of good strong material, would last for more than one generation. When it finally gave way after many years of use it would be replaced with as near a facsimile as the descendants of the early weavers could make. In this way, family patterns were kept alive down through the ages and became traditional. Sometimes the original patterns were wonderfully preserved, although they had been copied over and over again by many generations. These patterns would be copied with such feeling that the old familiar motif would emerge not as a fixed mold but as design with a freshness that made for style.

A saga-like quality characterizes the early Swedish weavings and embroideries. Peasant women transposed their Swedish legends into pattern designs of figures, ships, castles, stars, flowers, and trees. The tree has always been a favorite subject, since it dates back to early Scandinavian mythology, symbolizing life. Often only the leaves of the tree were used in a pattern intended to carry this symbol. Biblical figures also appeared. Over and over again the wise and foolish virgins with their oil lamps were woven into hangings and coverlets. "Adam and Eve" was an especially popular embroidery subject, the figures being worked in solid stitchery. The legendary subjects in parade hangings were the most decorative. In these hangings men stand guard at castle doors, lance in hand; Viking ships sail on woven waves, and men in armor ride charging horses. Some of the old textiles are delicately gay, breathing the atmosphere of a Swedish summer, with bright flowers as pattern material. Tulips and roses were used, but the lily motif, probably an inheritance from the Middle Ages, appeared most often. A brisk style characterizes fabrics with animal and bird designs. The animal most often used was the reindeer.

Because raw material and methods of workmanship naturally lend themselves to certain forms and combinations, the geometrical patterns are much like the ones met with all over the world. Besides the geometrical forms and the typically Swedish motifs, other motifs have been incorporated from time to time, some from old oriental textiles and some from European art in general. After the 16th century, European styles and fashions had little influence on Swedish textiles except in some embroideries and high warp tapestries in southern Sweden.

The seafaring people in the south of Sweden had contact with far distant lands, and as a result of this contact the natives of southern Sweden developed ideas derived from rococo designs of East Indian chinaware and flower designs from silk embroideries. And yet, these designs from the coastal districts were woven into their textiles with such originality that they became as truly national as designs produced by the more isolated people of the remote northern parts of Sweden.

On examining the old Swedish textiles an absolute sureness of technique becomes evident. This perfection of technique is proof of the early peasant's skillful craftsmanship, when one considers that the fabrics were woven on home-made looms with the simplest of implements and materials.

Swedish peasant textiles include all sorts of plaited and woven articles, and needle-work and embroideries made of linen or wool once belonging to an early peasant home. The prestige of the home was heightened by the number of fine fabrics and embroideries which it could display on occasions for celebration.

On such occasions, bright-colored cushions and pillows covered all the chairs and benches, with an especially fine one for the seat-of-honor. Hangings covering the walls and rafters gave the peasant's home a festive air entirely different from its everyday appearance. These wall hangings were either of linen — pattern-woven or embroidered — or of paper. Of the Swedish textiles, the white linen wall hangings that covered both walls and ceiling were the most remarkable. These hangings were fastened to the rafters and would extend down as far as the top of the wall; they were finished off with braided fringe. Where these hangings left off, others would be tacked to the wall, hanging down in turn as far as the built-in benches that lined the room. If the decorated hangings did not suffice to cover all the walls and the space right up to the ridgepole, ordinary bed sheets or the like were stretched across the bare spaces. All these textiles, together with the bed curtains, which nearly covered one of the long walls, made the room look like the inside of a tent.

This was the observance of a very old custom known to have been in use in northern countries since legendary times. During the Middle Ages and as late as the beginning of the 17th century, the dwellings of the higher classes were dressed up in very much the same way. In the peasant cottages in the south of Sweden, however, the custom persisted during nearly the whole of the 19th century. Elsewhere in Sweden the peasants would occasionally drape the room where the wedding party was to eat and dance with ordinary sheets, clothes, and covers. Sometimes borrowing from the neighbors would be necessary in order to provide enough linens to cover walls and ceiling.

The most interesting of the wall hangings are the huge ones from the two southern provinces of Skåne and Halland. These are woven of white linen with dark blue wool yarn inserted by hand as the linen is woven on the loom — a technique known as "*dukagång.*" Great care must be taken in even distribution of the yarn to give the fabric a uniform weight. Blue yarn was usually used, although in some rare cases red and even green yarn was added. The colored yarn formed the pattern. Since the pattern thread always went over the same warp thread and under others, the pattern became striped in the direction of the warp, but in such a way that the colored pattern threads were chiefly on the right side. The patterns were usually geometric or floral, but sometimes the women wove human figures, animals, and ships into them. In some cases the designs can be traced back to patterns found in fabrics of the 11th century.

Perhaps the best known hangings are the embroidered ones from another southern province, Blekinge. They are less old, and probably none antedates 1780. The last of them to be made were the work around 1865 of a little old peasant woman in Blekinge who embroidered and sold this sort of hanging. The embroidery was done on fine white linen in two shades of blue, rose, yellow, and red. The red and blue threads were often intertwined, giving a violet effect. The motifs—flowers, birds, and small ornamental borders—were copied by the peasants from embroideries favored by the Swedish upper classes. This special style of embroidery dates back to the wool-on-linen embroideries that were very much in fashion during the rococo times, and seems to have had its origin in England during the latter half of the 17th century. The patterns of these English embroideries were in turn inspired by floral textiles and prints which England imported from the Far East. By the time the fancy flowers of India and China had been copied into English embroideries, then copied in turn by the Swedish upper classes, and finally by the Blekinge peasants, they had gone through many changes, becoming as characteristic as patterns from other parts of Sweden.

In the more central province of Västergötland, hangings were less colorful, being made of all-white linen with insets of coarse white netting, but they were none the less decorative. The hangings were made as wide as the spaces between the rafters, so that they could be tacked to the rafters and extend all the way from the ridgepole to the walls. The patterns of the coarse white netting, which sometimes even included figures, stood out boldly against the dark timbers. Hangings of exactly this kind were used in the houses of the upper classes during the 15th and 16th centuries.

Another type of hanging was a large piece of material which covered the whole center of the ceiling and was fastened to huge hooks. This was appropriately called a ceiling dress.

Sometimes a big cloth was suspended above the feast table like a canopy. The four corners were fastened to rings in the rafters, and a red apple hung down from each of these corners. The center was caught up with a crown made of straw. This canopy was very often made of two widths of linen with a lace or net insertion. The most magnificent ones come from southern Sweden. These are made solely of white netting with darned patterns in blue and red cotton.

Each farm house would also have at least one fine tapestry, which would be stretched to the wall above the front door.

After the wedding, the holiday, or the Christmas festivities, the hangings would be taken down from walls and ceiling, to be rolled up and carefully stored away in great wooden chests, there to stay until the next happy occasion.

The wall hangings had their origin in Viking times, when maidens busied themselves at weaving while awaiting the return of their heroes. In northern and central Sweden the custom of hanging wall decorations was in favor until the peasant houses, with their exposed rafters and tiny windows, were replaced by two-storied houses with large windows and flat ceilings to cover rafters.

In the early peasant dwellings window curtains were unknown. The windows were small and few. Sometimes, however, a fringed valance would be hung at the top. Fringe would also be used to decorate shelves, cupboards, and even the moulding of the bedsteads and heavy beams. The thrifty peasant women made this fringe from warp ends. At the end of each linen web a part of the warp was left by which the web had been fastened to the loom. Cutting the linen from the loom left warp ends which could not be used in weaving. These threads were counted off in three or four strands and tied or braided together, making an elaborate fringe, sometimes with a tasseled effect.

Carpets were unknown in the early house. For special occasions the floor was usually strewn with fine-cut twigs of fir; sometimes rye straw was used. Broken bits of fir or straw were scattered about but did not completely cover the wide floor boards.

Below. Interior showing white linen and lace wall hangings from Västergötland. The floor is strewn with fine-cut twigs of fir, as was the custom.

Interior of a farmhouse from the south of Småland, in wedding dress, with wall hangings, woven or painted, and beam fringe.

This farm house from southern Småland adds to its decorations for a festive occasion a white ceiling dress.

Interior of an old and genuine cottage in Halland. Rölakan tapestries cover the benches and the walls behind them.

The sleeping places in old Swedish peasant houses were, in most cases, built into the wall, bunk style, and if they were not provided with shutters, they would have striped blue-and-white linen bed curtains that could be drawn. The beds were made up with bedstraw and several feather-beds, the higher the better, to show the wealth of the house. A coarse, heavy homespun covered the bedstraw, while the feather-beds had beautiful blue-and-white striped linen covers. On top of the bedding was a white linen spread which hung to the floor; it was either stretched out straight or arranged in pleated folds. Straight or pleated, it always ended in embroidery, fringe, or lace at the lower edge. On top of the white spread, a smaller gay-colored coverlet would be used; this extended only halfway to the floor, so that the decorative white under-spread would show. These colorful woolen coverlets were sometimes made of woven cloth, blue being a favored color, and were heavily embroidered in bright colored woolen yarns. More often, the patterns were woven into the material. The most striking of the woven covers are those done in double weave.

Double weave, as the name indicates, was woven in two layers of different colors and sometimes of two different kinds of materials. Patterns were formed by treading up the lower layer of the warp and separating it from the upper layer with a stick, after which the pattern was plucked up with a wooden sliver. This type of weaving is very old. It was much used during the Middle Ages in aristocratic homes of that time, not only in bed covers, but in wall hangings. These ancient fabrics had pattern designs of Viking ships with square sails and dragons. From the 13th century down to the 16th century, this weaving technique was highly practised. The early designs finally gave way to motifs of birds, animals, flowers, stars and figures bordered with geometric patterns. The later double weaving was done in two colors, one being the natural flax color, which made the patterns boldly stand out against a ground color of soft brick-red or black wool.

The white linen pillow-cases on the bed had a separate piece of embroidery, lace, or netting sewed on to the end of the case which showed toward the room. All this finery covered the ordinary bed clothes, which sometimes included a bed cover lined with sheepskin.

A white linen towel was hung over the striped

bed curtains at the head of each bed. This was very long and narrow, with embroidery and a fringed end, and it was purely ornamental, never being used as a towel. The pattern decoration of the towels matched the design of the pillow-cases and the embroidery on the part of the white spread that hung down under the colored bed-spread. These pieces formed a set, and in turn matched a towel that was always to be found just inside the entrance door, hanging from a small shelf fixed to the wall or fastened to the door post. This was also an ornamental towel and was made exactly like the towels hanging over the bed curtains. Each farm home used to have at least four of these towels, and they were used only at funerals, to carry out the coffin. The coffin had a cover, too, woven in somber colors. Many times the cover was especially made for the purpose, but very often it was the same cover which, on feast days, was used when laying the banquet table. However, most peasant homes boasted of special table-cloths for weddings and other festal occasions. These were gayer in color.

A great occasion was the annual visit of the clergyman to every farm in his parish. This called for a special table-cloth with a contrasting square woven into the center of the cloth; this was known as the clergyman's square and marked the place where the minister was to sit while he questioned not only every member of the family but all the servants and farm hands about the Scriptures. After this ordeal a great feast was spread.

Flemish weaving was introduced into Sweden in 1540, when King Gustav Vasa had stately tapestries made for the royal palace by weavers brought in from Flanders. Their magnificent high warp tapestries, with heavy fruit, leaves, and flower patterns, inspired the peasants to try this method of weaving on their own looms with their own simple materials. The cushions, hangings, and coverlets made by the peasants were delightfully naïve. The weavers did more than copy the fruit and flowers; they attempted animals, castles, and even figures dressed in their own native Swedish dress. Although this method of weaving certainly was not unknown in Sweden in ancient times, all the later *Flamsk* weaving in Sweden depends on European tapestry from the Renaissance and from the Baroque period.

Rölakan is ribbed like Flemish weaving. The name goes back to an ancient Swedish word, "back cloth," since the cloth was used as a covering for the backs of chairs and benches. *Rölakan* differs from Flemish weaving in that it is done with a horizontal warping, whereby the weft is shuttled or worked in by hand along a straight line and pressed together by the reed. In this way, too, the pattern tends to become more geometrical. The finest examples of *Rölakan* folk textiles come from the southern province of Skåne.

The English word for *rya* is "rug," but formerly in Sweden it always meant a bed cover with a knotted pile. In old Sweden the peasants slept between fur skins, even covering the straw pillows with fur. This was undeniably warm, but the skins became stiff and hard and the fur couldn't be washed. Because of this drawback, the peasants made covers that were just as warm and had the added advantage of being softer and washable. The early ones were made to simulate fur as nearly as possible. Wool plucked right from the sheep was used without first spinning it, and the natural colors of the wool, black, white, and grey, were worked into simple patterns in a very high pile. The wool was knotted in as weaving progressed. Since these coverlets were used with the pile side down, as the earlier fur skins were used, less care was given to the pattern than was given to the flat surface of the other side. On this side the initials of the owner were worked into the striped geometric design. The pile side had a lovely soft sheen and did indeed closely resemble fur.

In making later covers the wool was plunged into hot water before being worked into the *rya*. This of course shrunk, stiffened, and tightened the wool, and while it gave a more durable, lasting quality, the rugs were not as soft and glossy as the earlier ones.

About 1690 a new type of *rya* appeared. The wives and daughters of the burghers of Stockholm, and, after a time, women of similar class in the country, began to weave rugs with patterns copied from imported textiles with rich, Baroque floral patterns. The pile was made shorter and the rows of knots closer, producing a lighter-weight rug. The pile side was turned up to show the new patterns. If the weaver had no foreign Baroque fabric to copy, she took motifs from cross-stitch samplers and translated them into *rya* weaving. These motifs are easily recognized and, in the rugs, the effect is both amusing and charming. As it was employed only as a daytime spread, the *rya* lost its original useful function. The idea soon progressed from southern Sweden to northern Sweden and became the basis of the famous Swedish rugs of today.

Much work had to be done before the women could sit at their looms and weave lengths of linen and wool. Even before the early hawthorn was in bloom the peasants would go from farm to farm to help one another sow the flax. During the early spring sowing, both men and women worked in the fields, and as they toiled they drank a native ale with syrup, to offset the flax dust in their throats. All during the warm, light summer days that followed, the flax had to be tended with the greatest care. When finally it was ready to be harvested, neighbors would again help each other to get in the crop.

After the flax stalks had been harvested and rotted the peasant woman would grasp a bunch of them in her left hand and hold them over a scutching foot; her right hand would wield a wooden scutching knife, which came down on the stalks for blow after blow until the flax was worked free of all the slivers. After the woman had combed the honey-colored flax it was ready for spinning. The flax was wound around the distaff which was attached to the spinning wheel, and spinning began.

Spinning went faster and was less irksome if women could chat with their friends as they worked. Consequently it was a popular custom for married women to take their spinning wheels and gather at a neighboring farm, to spend the whole day spinning and exchanging bits of news. They would meet next at another farm, and so on as long as the spinning season lasted.

After the yarn was spun and wound into great hanks it was ready to be spooled on to the bobbins. Finally this warp was mounted on the loom, and weaving could begin.

Wool yarn was plucked by hand or cut with shears from the sheep. The carding was done with great care, first rough-carding and then fine-carding.

The ancient upright loom had a perpendicular warp, not the horizontal one that is used in Sweden today and has been in use since the early Middle Ages. In the former as well as in the latter, the wooden knife that pressed the weft threads into the warp may be regarded as the precursor of the weaver's beam.

The newly loomed linen was given many washings and bleachings. In order that the bleach might penetrate every thread, the peasant woman held the linen in the watery solution and beat it with a batlet. After the linen was dry, she rolled it on a cylindrical wooden roller which she rotated backwards and forward under a heavy wooden mangling board. The handle of the mangling board was usually shaped like a saddled horse, and the board would have carved designs of hearts and flowers and sometimes inscriptions, with its owner's initials and the date of her marriage. The batlet, distaff, scutching knife, and all her other weaving implements would be rich in chip carving, or painted with gay flowers. These were the gifts her husband had made and presented to her before she became his wife. When she accepted these gifts it meant, of course, that his attentions were welcome and he could begin courting her in earnest. No wonder then, that so much labor was expended on these weaving implements, for each was truly a labor of love. A richly carved but well-worn scutching knife tells a story of a young man who won his fair maiden.

Of course the betrothed maiden had a gift for her young man too. This was always a shirt, but she made it of her finest woven linen. An incredible amount of labor went into the embroidery of the collar and cuffs and even of the shirt front, although it was mostly covered by the waistcoat. This shirt was often made long before the girl had decided just whom she would marry; consequently it was always very large, with big billowy sleeves, so that it would fit her future husband be he tall, short, fat, or thin.

Besides the bridegroom's shirt, the girl was obliged to weave a great amount of linen and wool cushions, coverlets, and all the many things she would need in her new home. The number of these bore witness to the extent of her industry and to her capabilities as a future housewife. All this weaving had to be begun when she was a very young girl, so that her bride's chest would be filled when she reached a marriageable age. Such a chest might contain:

Several woven woolen coverlets
Embroidered and appliquéd cushions
Seat covers for all the chairs
Woven runners for the benches along the walls
Yards of fringed borders for the shelves and beams
Wall hangings to be hung at Christmas
Sheets, pillow cases and towels with matched embroidery
Linen table-cloths with braided fringe
An especially fine carriage cushion.

Mangling Board, top view. Unpainted and carved. Dated 1738. From Västmanland.

Below. Another Mangling Board, side view; the handle is a stylized horse. Dated 1775. Unpainted. Carved inscription: "If you are hardworking and industrious you will soon get married." From Bohuslän.

From drawings by the author.

Right. Distaff. This held the flax during the spinning. Carved and painted decorations. From Uppland.

Left. Distaff. Unpainted. From Uppland.

Both drawings by the author.

Of course some of the items would be made by other members of her family, to be given to her for her important chest.

The most beautiful of the pattern-woven linens is the well-known damask. Each farm would have its own special damask loom, but skilled workers would go from farm to farm setting up new warps. Since the manner of setting these warp threads determined the pattern to be woven, the setting would give the housewife a new pattern to add to her collection of patterns handed down in her family for generations. Wonderful names were given these damask patterns. One was "Billowing Waves"; another was "Snow Star." A typical table-cloth would have a small floral bouquet in the center, with possibly a double border pattern of vines.

Drill was used to weave simpler things in linen and half-linen, such as towels and some of the garments. Quilts of cotton and wool were also woven in this technique.

The very finest linen would go into making lovely caps and kerchiefs. In some provinces of the country the caps would be small and fitted to the head, always being trimmed in hand-made laces. In other provinces, they would be bonnets that

tied under the chin in huge bows, the ends of which would be bordered in the finest of bobbin lace.

All the garments the peasants wore were of their own hand-woven materials, made thin or heavy depending on the garment. The harvest costume was a smock of heavy linen, worn with a red girdle wound round the waist. The "church-going dress" was of much finer material. It was the custom for married women to wear elaborate headdresses to church, and these differed greatly in the various provinces. In the southern province of Blekinge an embroidered disc for the crown of the head was traditional. It was usually made of bright red woolen cloth and embroidered in silk, with gold lace and pewter paillettes. A wooden disc of the same size under the circular cloth kept it taut on the head. In the province of Skåne one skirt was not enough if a woman wished to be considered well-dressed. At least five or six skirts would be worn over the rough wool petticoat. The top skirt was always a little shorter than the second skirt, and this, in turn, a little shorter than the next, and so on. A woman could thus be sure that others knew how many skirts she possessed, for their number could be counted. The men were content to wear only three jackets

Right. Distaff. Carved and painted red. From Härjedalen.

Left. Distaff. Unpainted. From Uppland.

Both drawings by the author.

at a time, but each jacket had to be a bit shorter than the one under it, so that they, too, could be counted. Several pairs of trousers were worn with the jackets, in like manner.

Since it was the custom for guests to take knife, fork, and spoon with them to a feast, hanging purses were made to hold the utensils. Different provinces again had distinct styles, but whatever the shape, the purses were covered with bright bits of appliqué and stitchery.

It was custom also for a guest to bring a basket of food to the feast. Since everything had to have its own special embroidered cover, this basket had one too. "Leaves" of small pieces of linen, lace-bound and literally covered with openwork and satin stitch, gave the basket cover a special character.

A married woman always wore mittens to church. Since these had also been an engagement present from her husband, they usually had hearts-and-flower designs. Most of them were made of wool with silk embroidery, and they were sometimes fur-trimmed; if they were made of leather the embroidery was more conventionalized and might be done in pewter threads on the reindeer skin. The young man was not expected to make these—he would buy them at the village market place, where women would take any small items they had time to fashion after making all the things their own households needed. This work usually was in the form of knitting, which a woman could always have handy in her apron pocket, to work at during her "spare time"—a few minutes' rest from some other chore. During pauses from the heavy work in the fields she would knit a few rows on a pair of stockings or mittens. Her love of pattern could not let these things be done in plain, solid color. Rows of figures, stars, and animals would be knitted into the small pair of mittens, and of course the date and the owner's initials would be incorporated if she didn't intend to take them to market to sell. Natural white and black wool was her favorite combination. She also used this combination for her beautiful kerchiefs, worn with her Sunday dress, but here the combination was changed to black silk embroidered in snowflake and geometric patterns on fine white linen.

Many-colored wool embroidery on black, dark blue, green, or bright red homespun was done in all parts of Sweden. Cushions for chairs, carriages,

Right. Scutching Knife,
used in processing flax.
Carved and painted green
From Öland.

Left. Scutching Knife.
Carved and unpainted.
From Öland.

**Both drawings by the
author.**

and the saddle were decorated in stitchery. In the southern provinces of Skåne and Jämtland big covers for the bed and sleigh robes were also embroidered in bright colors on homespun. The patterns, composed chiefly of flowers, were very frequently arranged in a wreath with initials and date—four big flowers or plants ascending toward the center, one from each corner. This is the typical pattern of chair cushions of the Renaissance style. Baroque floral patterns with big, heavy flowers on thin, boldly curving stems were also used. The flowers have varied combinations of fillings and stitchery and were usually highly conventionalized. Animals and figures were popular motifs, as was Adam-and-Eve, with the Tree of Knowledge and the serpent.

The smaller cushions, appliquéd in glowing colors against dark grounds, gave an almost jeweled mosaic effect. Patterns would be astonishingly well conventionalized. Little separate pieces of bright cloth would be appliquéd to the cushion top and sewed on with bright-colored threads. These pieces would be outlined with a row of chain stitch and sometimes rows of contrasting colored threads of chain stitch. Often the complete pattern was carried out in row after row of this oldest of stitchery patterns. Some cushion tops were patchwork.

In southern Sweden the cushions were frequently made in pairs and generally were used as bride's cushions, being brought to the church by two outriders who carried them hanging down from the knob of the saddle-bow by a leather loop at the center of one side of the cushion, provided for this purpose. In the church they were placed at the foot of the altar rails for the bridal couple to kneel on during the marriage ceremony. The bride's pillow would have the year of the wedding and her initials; if her name was Karin and her father's given name was Per, the initials would be K.P.D. (Karin PersDotter), the D standing for daughter. If the man's cushion top had the letters B.N.S., the S stood for son, and his name might have been Bengt Nils-Son. On pillow tops these initials would be worked usually in cross-stitch.

Besides the wedding cushions, many other textiles were so marked, the initials denoting ownership and not necessarily the maker. Often we find an added H before the initials. This stood for *"Hustru"*, meaning a married woman. The letter J before the initials means *"Jungfru,"* and conveyed that the initials were those of an unmarried girl. This was the accepted way of signing all things made by hand.

14

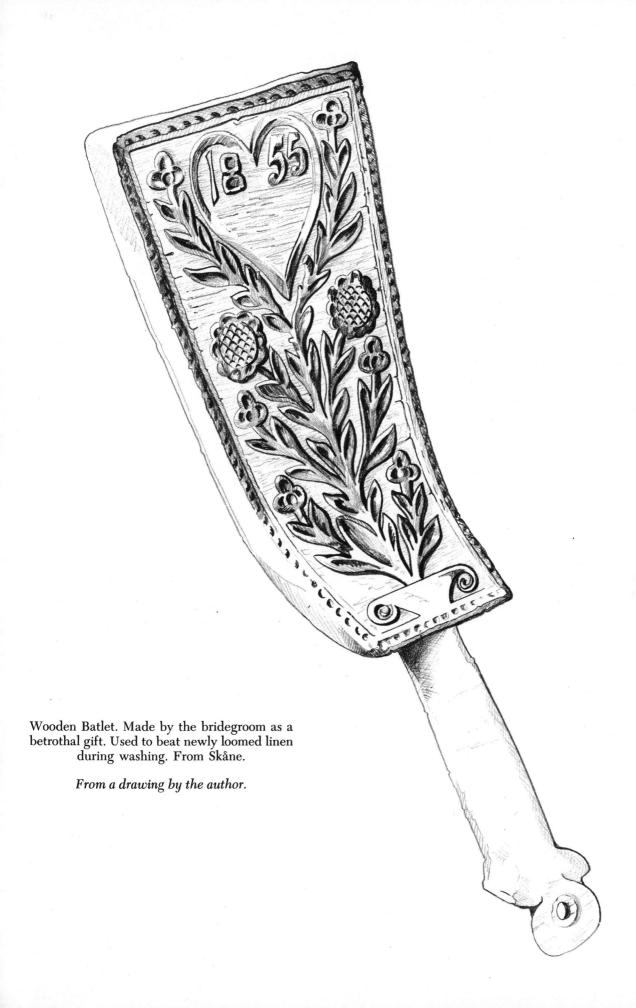

Wooden Batlet. Made by the bridegroom as a
betrothal gift. Used to beat newly loomed linen
during washing. From Skåne.

From a drawing by the author.

The natural colors of the wool—white, black, and grey—were sometimes used, but more often the Swedish love of color demanded strong, clear dyes. Many distinct hues were obtained by dyeing with indigenous vegetables, with leaves, roots, herbs, and rock-moss. Indigo was imported for blue and cochineal for crimson. In the very early days, linen was dyed only blue or yellow, as the art of dyeing flax yarn red was still unknown. Cotton was not in use at all before the end of the 18th century, and even then only in small quantities, mostly bright-red cotton yarn for embroidery on linen. When cotton finally became common, in the 19th century, factory goods made their way into homes in nearly all parts of the country. There ensued a period of decline for the domestic textile art. By 1850 the old home industry had come to an end.

When industry took over the manufacturing of textiles, old patterns were sometimes imitated, but in general the special character of the old homespun fabrics was lost. By the end of the 19th century, however, the home craft (*Hemslöjd*) movement had revived the old Swedish textile art. Weavers went back to their looms and again wove lengths of linen and wool in the traditional patterns, using the ancient techniques.

Today this well organized *Hemslöjd* Association is responsible for the wealth of fine homespun textiles to be found in Sweden. Realizing that imitation often leads to laxity, the modern artists create fresh designs but strive to keep them characteristic of different provinces and guided by old traditions. The home weavers are supplied with these designs and are commissioned to make as many pieces or yards as the *Hemslöjd* Association requires.

The ancient techniques are kept alive. *Rya* rugs much like the old ones which resembled fur are made today. The decorative double weaving is still produced, especially in the western coastal districts and in the North. Only in Sweden has damask weaving been kept as a handicraft. Flemish weaving is still practiced, as are the many methods used in the old days.

Besides the many fine homespun and embroidered textiles to be found in *Hemslöjd* shops throughout Sweden today, there are many, fine modern fabrics. Although some of them show no derivation from the traditional, other bold, modern designs may be traced directly to the patterns of the old home industry. In either case, the old methods of weaving are employed, and this modern conception of design using ancient techniques gives the textiles a stylization that is unique. Brisk, modern handblocked designs on linen are created by artists working independently in their own workshops.

Ecclesiastical textile art has always been of great importance in Sweden. Few countries possess such rich church textiles from early times, and the elaborate ones being made today are of the same high level.

Machine-made textiles, an industry that ranks third in importance after iron and timber, are of especially high quality because of the close cooperation that exists in Sweden between artist and manufacturer.

Dukagång Wall Hangings. They are typical of Blekinge in being made to hang the "long way," corresponding in width to the space between two rafters. The white linen, woven in red and blue, is less closely covered with pattern than those of some other provinces. Both belonged to the same household, each showing the same set of initials of husband and wife.

Left. Hanging woven in "krabbasnår" technique, which allowed a few details to be embroidered after the main part of the pattern was woven into the white linen. In dark blue, rose, and light red. From Blekinge.

Above. Detail from Wall Hanging. White linen with pattern in dukagång in dark blue, red, and green wool. The lion motif shows it to have been originally copied from some ancient fabric, like so many other designs from Skåne. Dated 1806.

Below. Detail from white linen Wall Hanging with dukagång pattern in dark blue wool. The pattern may be traced back to 11th-century fabrics. From Skåne.

Above. Detail of Wall Hanging from Skåne in dukagång weave; pattern in dark blue wool and white linen. The castle and horseman are common patterns in European folk art, especially in eastern Europe, and are to be found in Italy as well; they come originally from the Orient, like so many other textile designs. In dukagång technique they have a special Scandinavian character, not only in the weaving, but in the addition here of the added row of Biblical virgins with their lamps, and the eight-pointed star.

Right. Detail of a dukagång Wall Hanging. The pattern is dark blue wool woven into white linen. The small animal under the deer is the fabulous "basilisk," which, like the unicorn, found its way into heraldry.

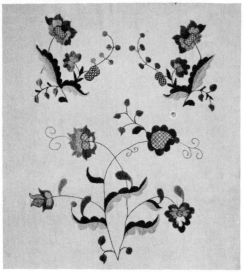

Above, left. Wall Hanging from Blekinge, embroidered with two shades of blue, rose, and a little yellow, on white linen. Dated 1839, with a woman's initials, I.P.D.

Above. Blekinge Wall Hanging embroidered in light and dark blue, red, and yellow, on white linen.

Left. Detail of embroidered Wall Hanging from Blekinge.

Double weave Bed Coverlet, in natural-colored linen and brick-red wool. B.N.D. made it in 1781, and her husband's initials, O.P.S., are also woven into the bottom edge. Here again we find the Biblical virgins with their lamps, dressed in Swedish native dress. The peacock is another popular motif, as is the star. The border repeats IHS, the traditional monogram for Christ. From the province of Bohuslän.

Above. Detail of linen embroidered Beam or Shelf Hanging from the southern province of Halland. The cross-stitch pattern embroidered in bright red cotton in 1864 has now faded to a lovely soft rose.

Embroidered pieces for pillow-cases. In the northern province of Hälsingland pillows were made long, for two. The embroidery, usually in red cotton, was on separate pieces, sewed to the end of the pillow-case. The top one is a fine cross-stitch pattern of hearts and flowers; little "leaves" hang from some of the hearts. The two pieces at the bottom are worked in free satin stitch and stem stitch.

Right. Towel ends embroidered in rose cotton thread on white linen. From Hälsingland. It was the custom to hang one at the head of each bed over the bed curtains as a decoration, a matching one being hung by the door as a symbol of hospitality. Dated 1883.

Left. Towel ends with red outline and satin stitch embroidered floral design, from Hälsingland. Hung from the doorpost as a decoration only. Matching towels were hung from each bedstead.

Both towels were initialled by the maidens who embroidered them, the preliminary "I" signifying Iungfru in the old spelling.

Section of Bedstead Hanging with red cross-stitch. From Hälsingland. The peasant women never stamped their patterns, always painstakingly counting each thread as they worked in the tiny crosses.

Right. Small hanging "leaves" adorn the corners of this linen cloth, used to protect and dress up the basket or bowl of food which each guest took to festivals as a gift. It comes from Skåne.

Blue woolen homespun Coverlet, embroidered in woolen yarn in black, white, pink, and yellow. These covers were woven in two parts and seamed down the center. From Skåne.

Chair Cushion from the northern province of Jämtland made in 1769. Symmetrical patterns of large flowers growing from a single stem are characteristic of Jämtland. Unlike the patterns from southern Sweden, those of the northern provinces have less space-filling detail.

Chair Cushion, embroidered in wool on linen canvas, from the northern province of Härjedalen. It is worked in a special kind of close cross-stitch using one short and one long stitch in each cross. The design is worked in red, blue, yellow, and white with dark brown outlining against a solid cross-stitched ground. Like most of the cushions it had a tassel of bright-colored rags in each of the corners.

This gay Chair Cushion comes from Skåne. It was embroidered in 1789 in bright red, blue, yellow, and white on black woolen cloth. A pencil sketch of a Detail is shown on page 16.

Cushions for chair, made of black woolen fabric embroidered in red, green, and white. It has the husband's initials, P. I. S., and the wife's, E. I. D., and the date 1815. For a wedding or other important event, every chair had its own elaborate cushion, afterwards stored away.

Left. Dark brown embroidered Chair Cushion from Skåne, 1813.

Below, center. Carriage Cushion from Skåne, embroidered in red, white, yellow, and bright blue on black woolen cloth. Dated 1795. Many things inspired the peasant woman who made this ambitious design. She not only included herself, four times repeated, in her native dress, plus bridal crown, but symbolized the church in which she was married, supported by boxed-in tulips, held by traditional reindeer which stand on floral scrolls. The large flowers in each corner and the floral wreath with many initials suggest Renaissance influence. The flowers at the top and bottom have an Eastern air, probably the inspiration of a textile from England imported originally from India or China. Filling the ground almost completely with flowers was probably suggested by a Flemish tapestry she had glimpsed.

Left. Sleigh or Carriage Cushion probably made as a wedding gift. The wedding couple stand hand-in-hand under a big bridal crown. Floral wreaths enclose the familiar reindeer. Dated 1787. From Skåne.

Bride's Cushions were made in pairs for the marrying couple to kneel on during the ceremony in church. The patterns included the year and were identical except for the initials of bride and groom, respectively.

Right. Bride's Cushion once belonging to Elizabeth Olofsdotter of Skåne.

Above. Bride's Cushion from Halland. The pattern of four large flowers ascending from each of the four corners, with a floral wreath in the center, holding the date of the wedding and the initials, is typical of the Renaissance style.

Right. Bride's Cushion from Skåne. M.O.D. shyly worked a tiny heart between two love birds. Mostly in bright red, yellow, green and blue on a very dark brown woolen cloth. The fringe picks up all the colors.

Above. Carriage Cushion from Skåne with popular motif, "The Fall of Man". White-faced Eve, holding a fig-leaf branch and flanked by a reindeer, accepts a red apple from the serpent. Adam, with the King of Beasts beside him, stands on the other side of the Tree of Knowledge, whose roots grow into space-filling flowers. Made of wool with a linen warp, the pattern is entirely of inverted rows of stem stitch. On the extreme right is the creation of Eve from the sleeping Adam, and on the far left, the expulsion from the Garden.

Left. Dark blue woolen Carriage or Sleigh Cushion, embroidered in woolen yarn, from Skåne. Its creator, in tracing her initials, unwittingly reversed them.

Carriage Cushion embroidered on linen. A Flemish weaving pattern was probably the inspiration. A unicorn in front of a tree was a favored motif. From Skåne.

Left. Carriage Cushion from Skåne in "rölakan" weave. This pattern, typical of this province, makes varied use of the eight-pointed star. The method of weaving and the materials lend themselves to geometric patterns. The colors are always strong—very dark blue, bright blue, red, yellow, and green, with white for small accents.

Right. Parts of two Bed Covers, woven by the same weavers and probably at the same time, in 1781, perhaps by two sisters, AMD and TMD. The Tree, symbolizing life, the reindeer with birds, the horseman—each motif framed by birds inside an octagon—were popular derivations from Eleventh-century originals, in this type of low-warp tapestry weaving. From Skåne.

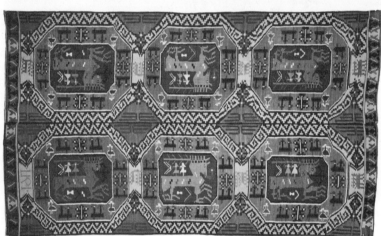

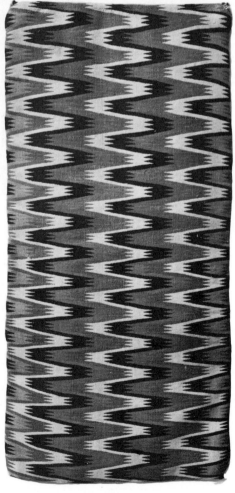

Top. Flamsk vävnad (Flemish weaving) Carriage Cushion from Skåne. The lion motif, and castles in the background, with large flowers inspired by the Flemish royal tapestries of 1540 Copied on home-made peasant looms, a naïve charm replaced magnificence.

Above. Rölakan Coverlet, dated 1761, from Skåne. This is the familiar "Red Deer" pattern. The center deer holds a lily in his mouth.

Right. "Lightning Pattern" Carriage Cushion in rölakan weave. From Skåne.

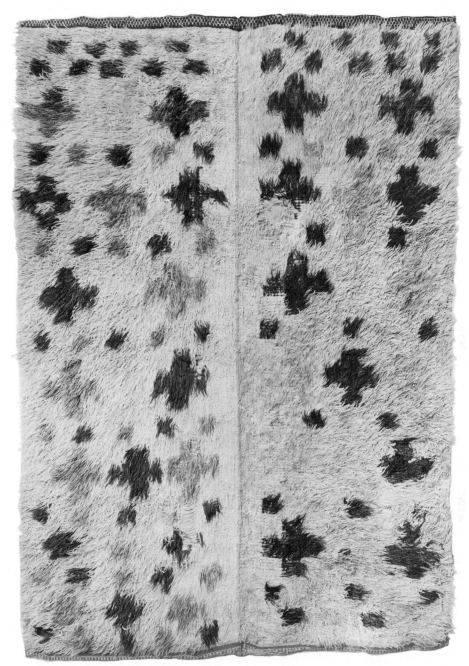

"*Rya,*" from the province of Småland. The pattern of crosses arranged in rows may have derived from the Medieval Cross pattern. Wool plucked from black sheep was used for the dark crosses, and for the lighter crosses wool from grey sheep. The background was made of wool from white sheep. As weaving progressed, the unspun wool was tied with an oriental knot into a blue-and-white-checked linen canvas. The Swedish word "*rya*" means rug in English, but formerly in Sweden it always meant a bed cover with a knotted pile. These shaggy covers, made to replace the earlier fur-skin bed covers and closely resembling fur in their lovely, soft sheen, are the basis of the famous Swedish floor rugs of today.

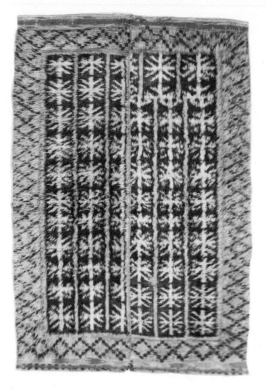

Above, left. Peasant *Rya* Coverlet from Jämtland. The design is in mellow yellows against soft dark green, with black used in the center of each diamond.

Above, right. Rya with a knotted pile on both sides, made in 1805. The pattern, mostly in red, is on a black ground and is typical of the islands just outside Stockholm, in Uppland province.

Left. Rya, from Blekinge. The repeated motif may derive from simplified tree forms.

Right. Rya, made for the higher classes. It comes from Ångermanland, in the northern part of Sweden, and is made of one piece, with a rather short pile. It was probably made at the time of the vogue for using these covers as daytime spreads only, with the pile side up, to show the pattern. Imported fabrics and prints were the inspiration of patterns such as this one. The rich floral Baroque style differentiates these covers sharply from the peasant examples.

Left. Rya, made in 1758 by a peasant woman of Bred, Uppland. She, too, used this as a daytime spread and was inspired by patterns in covers made for the higher classes. Not having a Baroque brocade to copy, however, she could only follow the general plan of a center design with a floral border. Patterns from her cross-stitch towel designs were copied into the pile pattern, along with floral embroidery patterns, and fowl and animals were used to fill in spaces. Although this *rya* comes from the central province of Uppland it has the crossed-arrows emblem of Dalarna province, used also in the textile patterns of many other provinces.

Mittens knitted in natural black and white wool, from the province of Dalsland. Only slightly less than actual size.

Below. Knitted into the small space was a steepled church, with windows and a door provided with a knob, a ladder to Heaven with angels in mid-air, birds, animals, flowers, and stars.

Above. Eight-pointed stars are knitted into the tip, and among a diversity of motifs are the Biblical virgins, both wise and foolish. Two rows of figures circle the thumb. The date, 1855, and the owner's initials complete the pattern.

Right. Holiday mittens which belonged to Peruilla Trulsdotter of Skåne in 1784. Made of black woolen cloth with silk embroidery in yellow, green, blue, and red silk.

Above. Wool Purse, appliquéd and embroidered. A ribbon ran through the clasp and tied around the woman's waist. From Dalarna.

Right. Headdress, seen from above, for a married woman from Blekinge province. Silk embroidery with gold lace and paillettes on red wool.

Above. A Purse worn hung from the waist. Black cloth with appliqué in red, green, and yellow, and embroidered in blue, white, and yellow silk. For festive occasions or church-going. From Dalarna.

Above. A church-going Purse which hung from the waist by red and white woven ribbons. The hearts and flower pattern was appliquéd to white leather in red and green cloth. If worn to a feast, it would hold the owner's knife, fork and wooden spoon. From Dalarna.

Left. Sash of red cloth with embroidery, decorated with silver lace and bordered in green ribbons and blue silk fringe. Dated 1762, with the initials N.B.D.

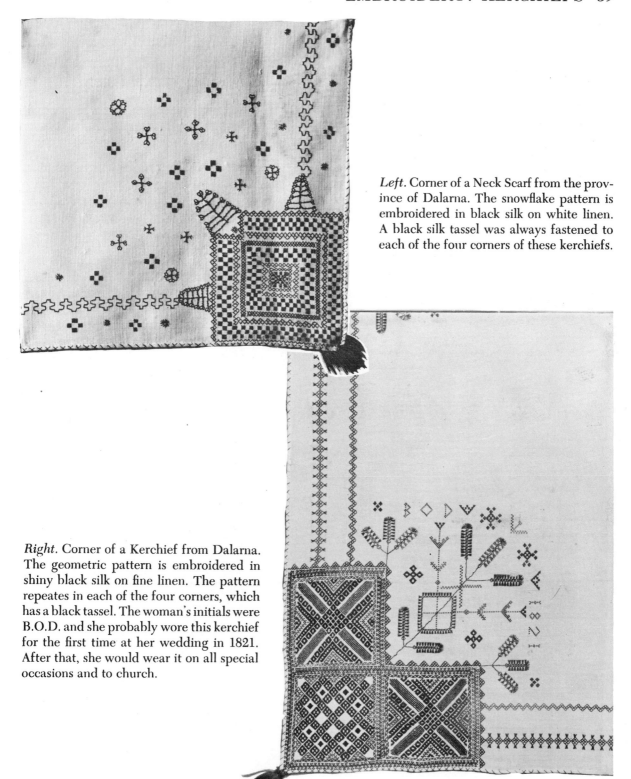

Left. Corner of a Neck Scarf from the province of Dalarna. The snowflake pattern is embroidered in black silk on white linen. A black silk tassel was always fastened to each of the four corners of these kerchiefs.

Right. Corner of a Kerchief from Dalarna. The geometric pattern is embroidered in shiny black silk on fine linen. The pattern repeats in each of the four corners, which has a black tassel. The woman's initials were B.O.D. and she probably wore this kerchief for the first time at her wedding in 1821. After that, she would wear it on all special occasions and to church.

Left. Kerchief from Dalarna with fanciful pattern embroidered in glossy black silk on fine white linen, with initials A.O.D. and the date 1851. Since the neck cloths were worn folded into a triangle, "A.O.D." probably decided to embroider only the part that would show.

Right. End of Towel from Halland province, embroidered in red cotton on white linen. These long narrow towels were always to be found just inside the entrance door, hanging from a small shelf or from the doorpost. In some provinces they also decorated the bedsteads. The towel was never used except when a funeral took place. Then the coffin was borne from the house resting on four of these long white linen strips.

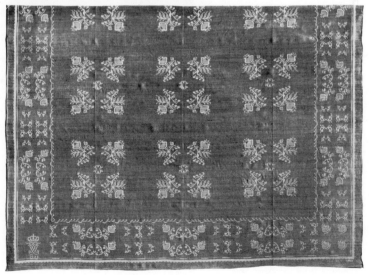

Top. A Cushion of present-day execution, woven for the Hemsloyd Association, an adaptation of the type of traditional carriage-cushion design shown on page 32. *Center.* An ecclesiastical Damask designed at Licium and woven by Hemsloyd craftsmanship. *Right.* Damask Table-cloth executed for the Hemsloyd in Ångermanland, a replica of a traditional pattern.

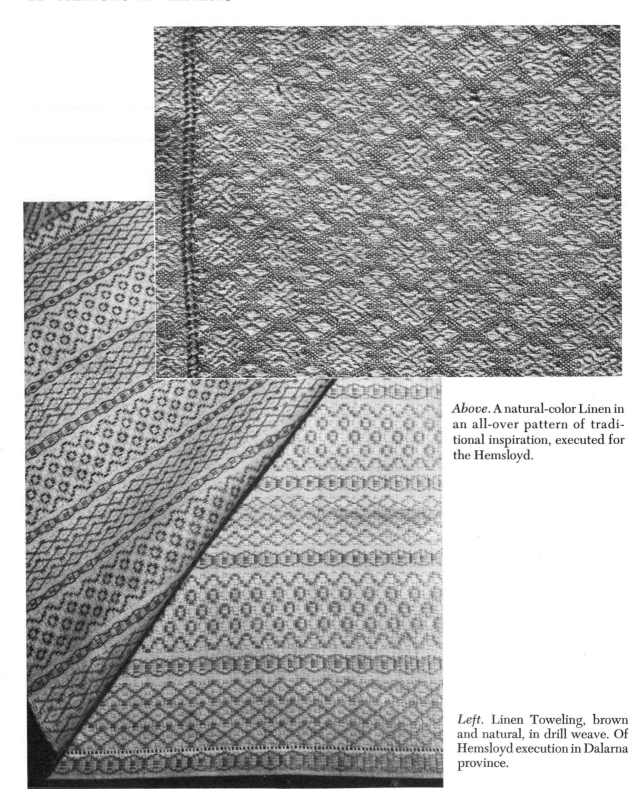

Above. A natural-color Linen in an all-over pattern of traditional inspiration, executed for the Hemsloyd.

Left. Linen Toweling, brown and natural, in drill weave. Of Hemsloyd execution in Dalarna province.

The "Fuchsia" Cushion at top is made in Värmland. In the Cushion at center, the four large flowers, executed in solid stitchery, are repeated in smaller scale in the horse, also in solid stitchery. Patterns are of traditional inspiration. The lower Cushion shows a modernized version of traditional birds and flowers.

Left. A straw "Crown," the function of which is described on Page 7. Dating from Viking times, the present-day versions, such as that shown here, are still used for Christmas decoration.

Below. The traditional knitted Mittens shown on Page 36 find their present-day counterpart in these Hemsloyd examples.

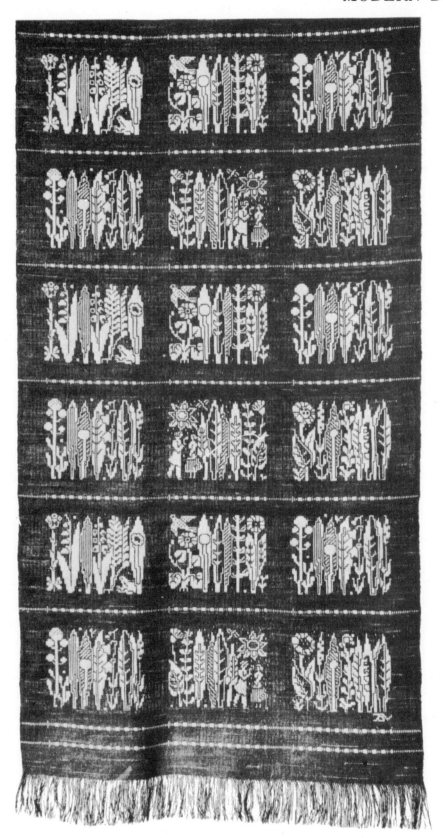

Hanging, widely exhibited, a distinguished example of the work of the Weaving School of Johanna Brunsson. Established in 1878 at Tångelanda and moved to Stockholm in 1889, it is today a very famous school to which entry is eagerly sought. A Coverlet in traditional double weave is shown on page 21.

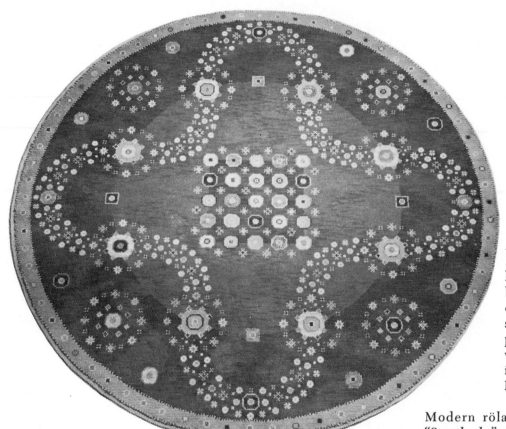

A beautiful modern *Flossa* Rug, with a knotted pile like *Rya*, but woven more closely and with a shorter pile. No important detail repeats without modification, in a design by Barbro Nilsson.

Modern rölakan Rug done in "*Svartbroka*," which denotes the predominance of black in a design with other colors. Here, in a design by Ann-Mari Lindbom, it is combined with red and white.

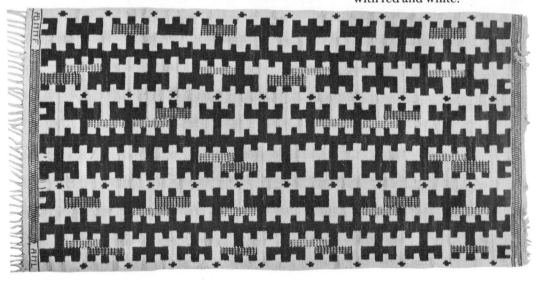

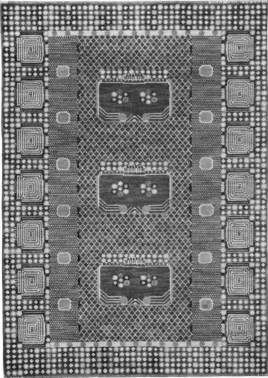

Top, left. Flossa Rug in which Marianne Richter has modernized the traditional Tree-of-Life motif. Woven in yellow and browns, it is aptly named "Yellow Trees."

Top, right. "Hopskotch" is the translation of the name of this whimsical Rug designed by Ann-Mari Lindbom. It is woven in the older *rya* technique, with a long shaggy pile.

Left. Motifs of the sea were used in this *Flossa* Rug designed by Barbro Nilsson for the Textile Research Institute in Gothenburg. Here are fishnets, sand, stones, and crabs.

Left. Hand-printed fabric designed by Sven Markelius for NK:s Textile Workshop, Stockholm.

Below. "Nursery Hearts," a Linen printed in pink, light yellow, and turquoise. Designed by Astrid Sampe-Hultberg for NK:s Textilkammare (Textile Workshop), Stockholm.

Bottom. Block-printed fabric using seven colors on black ground. Designed by Joseph Frank of Svenskt Tenn, Stockholm.

Above. "Once Upon a Time", a hand-printed fabric designed by Sven-Erik Skawonius for NK:s Textile Workshop, and intended for upholstering a modern sofa. The upper band of design covers the back, the lower band the seat. The floral and animal motifs are modernized traditional.

Left. Sofia Widén's design for Textilatelier Licium, Stockholm. A fabric named "Lapponia", of Lapp motifs—the midnight sun, northern lights, great bonfires, roaming and corralled reindeer, lakes, rivers, and rocky mountaintops.

Above. Modern printed Linen designed by
Stig Lindberg, who has done distinguished
work in ceramic design.

Right. Printed in ten colors on a white ground
—the design of Joseph Frank, of Svenskt Tenn.
The chair in the foreground shows the amaz-
ing scale.

Above. Detail of an Altar-cloth designed by Greta Mörk and embroidered on silk by Gurly Hillbom.

Left. Embroidered detail of a Bishop's Cape designed by Märta Afzelius.

Below. Wall Hanging, with Detail shown at left. Designed by Märta Afzelius and embroidered on handwoven linen.

All three designed for Licium, Stockholm.

 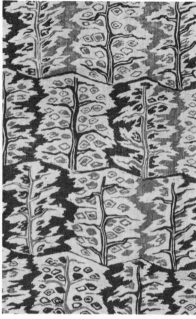 

Left to right. "Stockholm" and "Oak Trees," by Sofia Widén. "Tales," a nursery-rhyme fabric by Susan Gröndal. All three for Licium.

Below, left to right. A spring-flower design by Joseph Frank of Svenskt Tenn. "Fishes," by Tyra Lundgren, and "Gingerbread Men," by Susan Gröndal; both for Licium.

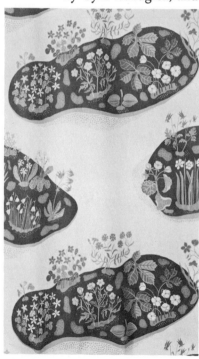  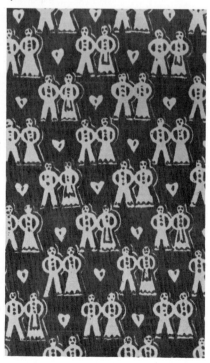

Above. Three modern fabrics designed by Lisbet Jobs.

Below. The first fabric is designed by Lisbet Jobs; the second, "Midsummer," and third are by Gocken Jobs.

All designed for NK:s Textile Workshop.

Above. Theatre Curtain.

Right. Hand-blocked Linen, "Cats."

Both made by Elsa Gullberg; designed by Vicke Lindstrand.

CHAPTER III

CERAMICS

THE fact that ceramics occupy the most prominent place amongst archeological findings is very probably due to the perishability of wood, for in olden days most of the household utensils used in the Swedish peasant home were made of wood. Although there is ample evidence of the early existence of ceramics, it is only natural that the peasant woman depended almost entirely on vessels and utensils of wood or birchbark for daily use. The great wooded areas furnished the material. Her men folk were expert in whittling and carving, and could fashion any size or shape of vessel she might need. Ceramic pieces, on the other hand, had to be bought. She cherished them and took great pride in having as large a number as possible exposed to view on shelves along the walls. Only on special occasions were the earthenware plates taken from their racks and piled high with fancy cakes for expected guests.

Not until the 17th century did these pottery plates, bowls and other pieces make their appearance. The nobility and the townspeople of Sweden were beginning to use glazed ware, and the peasants, as usual, were emulous of the culture of the upper classes.

A brown earthenware dish with yellow and green line ornamentation, dated 1644, is one of the oldest pieces of Swedish pottery. An earthenware bottle dated 1682 is another notable old ceramic object. Patterns of scanty lines in yellow or yellow-and-green on the simple brown dishes may have been an attempt to imitate basket-weaving patterns of that time, and these vessels were given the name of "*snörkeramik*" (lace ceramic) because their scratched line patterns did in fact seem to represent basket-weave lacings. A bowl dated 1711 shows that this style was still flourishing in the beginning of the 18th century, although by that time dishes with yellow glaze and decoration in red and green were beginning to appear.

A great deal of the earthenware that the peasants took such joy in was made in northern Skåne and the province of Halland and sold by the potters at the great fairs in Småland. The products of the Hallandian "pottery towns" were spread widely into all parts of the country, and earthenware dishes with tulip patterns which are found throughout large districts of western Sweden seem to have come from these towns. The towns of Kalmar, Stockholm, Uppsala, Gävle, and others were known locally as "*lergökastäderna*," or "clay-cuckoo towns" because of their manufacture of toy ocarinas in bird form. The pottery towns were seats of great pottery guilds.

It is difficult to detect any special local characteristics in the early pottery. In fact, there is a great deal of uniformity in early ceramics from all parts of Sweden, and they bear a resemblance to wares from other European countries, Dutch and German influence being the strongest.

By the middle of the 18th century it was usual for ceramics to be wholly glazed with a highly plastic and fairly pure grayish-white clay, and decorated with flowers and figures painted in green, yellow, red, and lilac-black. In the same period, all-black and all-green ceramics began to appear.

By the 19th century a more highly glazed pottery and simple flint porcelain had become comparatively common in the rural homes, and with the passage of time the coarse earthenware was used only for storage and daily utility purposes.

The 18th century earthenware shows a great variety of distinct motifs. Dishes of course were the most suitable objects for decorating. Stylized tulips, roses, birds and figure motifs were skillfully painted on them in strong, sure lines. Often a bold decoration was obtained by means of floating colors. On yellow dishes there is very often an arrangement of dotted lines in concentric circles around the central motif. Incised designs on yellow-over-brown dishes revealed the brown under-substance.

Special dishes were made to hold cooked fish. In the center of the dish was a small round depression to hold the sauce, and the fish, cut into pieces, would be arranged on the dish around the sauce holder.

Small bowls were usually made with handles so that they could be hung by the hearth. Bowls, tureens, and bottles more or less imitated forms and decorations associated with the better types of faience. Clay oil-lamps were made only in the coastal districts. The most common type of candlestick, made of calcined unglazed clay, took a form derived from the triangle. If the candlestick had any ornamentation at all it was usually a simple design of scratched lines.

Another important aspect of the potter's craft was the making of tiles for stoves. Porcelain stoves were never used in the smaller Swedish peasant dwellings where the hearth was depended on for cooking and heating. The tile stoves were used in town homes and official residences, and the most common type had a tile of a single color with a speckled effect, usually in green or yellow. These may still be seen in many of the older buildings in Stockholm and other cities. Another impressive

tile stove was made entirely of pure white tiles, but these white stoves belong to the second half of the 19th century.

The earliest faience from the Rörstrand factory, which was founded in Stockholm in 1726, followed the Dutch style of using decorative motifs of a Chinese character. Rococo style gradually gained preference over the Delft forms and finally supplanted them. Splendid bowls and dishes with Swedish inscriptions resulted. A characteristic inscription translates "May Sweden's flags be always blowing and Sweden's cradles always going."

By 1758 another faience factory was established near Stockholm, the factory of Marieberg. The competition between this factory and Rörstrand brought the Swedish manufacture of faience to a high degree of artistic achievement. Marieberg faience was characterized by all-white objects with the surface left unpatterned. If a design was wanted, it was applied in black; this black-on-white faience became the Marieberg factory's best known output. Not until 1827 was another important faience factory established, that of Gustavsberg. Toward the end of the century, in 1886, the Upsala-Ekeby factory was founded.

The Marieberg factory ceased operation in 1788, but the Rörstrand Porcelain Factory, the Gustavsberg Porcelain Factory, and Upsala-Ekeby A.-B. have grown into establishments of great importance, and objects currently produced from these factories are to be highly cherished.

Besides the factory-made faience, many decorative hand-turned pieces are produced by independently working faience-makers who are always careful to work in accordance with the character of their material. Sparing stylization rather than the decoration of earlier forms characterizes the more modern ceramics, resulting in highly attractive pieces in which there is no sacrifice of the suitability of the objects for their intended use.

The symbolical Tree-of-Life in the free style of northern Hälsingland province. On this yellow plate, dated 1698, brown and green are used and alternately repeated in the rim border of loosely formed ovals. These ovals might well be the forerunner of the dotted rim patterns in later dishes. Simple brown vessels with scanty line ornamentation preceded earthenware plates of this type.

Plate dated 1699 from Mora, Dalarna. The Tree-of-Life design is executed in brown and green on this yellow plate, which is one of the earliest pieces to be so decorated.

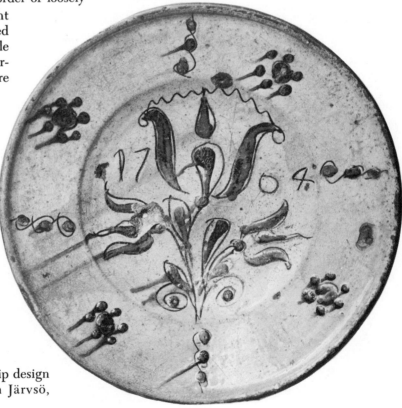

Yellow plate with bold tulip design in brown and red. From Järvsö, Hälsingland. Dated 1704.

Plate from Delsbo, Hälsingland. Dated 1728. Red, green, and yellow-green on a yellow ground, in a sturdy tulip design.

Three colors, green, red, and brown,were used in this elaborately designed Plate from Revinge, Halland, dated 1739. The familiar reindeer motif is surrounded by a floral pattern. Probably made as a wedding gift, as the bride's initials and traces of the groom's are discernible.

Plate from Dalarna. Dated 1731. The three tulips in the center and the seven evenly spaced tulips of the rim border give this dish a pleasing orderliness. Yellow dots accent the brownish red tulips. Green leaves.

The center design, which holds the date 1746, is reminiscent of the painted designs of earlier wooden drinking vessels (see page 158 under Wood). This dish from Dalarna, using traditional design material, has a purely Swedish character.

Plate from Knäred, Halland. Dated 1779. Red and green were the colors of the wide-eyed, speckled bird about to perch on a conventionalized tulip leaf. The stem of the tulip follows the curve of the plate and is repeated in a running curved stem on the inside border which is topped with a highly stylized tulip. The bold treatment of the outer edge repeats the running stem and adds an unusual decorative note.

Plate from Arbrå, Hälsingland. Stylized yellow and brown tulips with crossed green leaves seem to support the date 1791.

Plate made in Delsbo, Hälsingland, in 1788. Forever emulous of the higher classes, the potter depicted a lady in flowing gown with outstretched hand. The colors are brown, dark green, brownish green and yellow.

This later, rimmed Plate from Delsbo, Hälsingland, with its well-spaced band design, has the peacock motif turned and repeated in its entirety, even to the date, 1865. There is charm in the choice of colors, brown and yellow on a paler yellow ground.

This Fish Dish from Västergötland, dated 1724, has a simple pattern of red tulips with green leaves on a yellow ground. Since fish has always been a large part of the Scandinavian diet, special dishes were made on which to serve it. The fish was cut into pieces and placed around the small basin in the center, which held a sauce.

18th-century earthenware Porringer from Småland with design of brown and yellow tulips and green leaves. Such tureens held the traditional gift of barley porridge taken to great feasts by the guests. Since most porringers were made of wood, this earthenware tureen is rare.

Right. Form and decoration of this 1694 Vase from Småland show an attempt by the potter to imitate faience used by the higher classes. The vase has a yellow surface, with green, brown, and red used in the design.

Below. The Puzzle Jug was the medium of a prank played at feasts. Each farm house owned one and guests were expected to drink from it.

Drinking from the puzzle jug was always a feat. In the Jug shown, six of the pipes at top had to be closed with the fingers, leaving one open to drink from. The jug had to be tilted in such a way that the beverage in the bottom would flow through the hollow handle and the thick hollow rim and finally out the one pipe left open. If this was not executed properly, the joke was on the unlucky victim who was drenched by the contents. The jugs were made in different shapes and "puzzles," but the principle was the same. Many of them were of wood. This one is dated 1750 and comes from the province of Småland.

Left. Deep greenish brown Drinking Bowl with pale green pattern. Made in Hälsingland in 1680. It was conveniently held by two handles, one in the shape of a head, the other an open handle so that the bowl could be hung on the wall when not in use.

Above. Yellow Dish with vigorously drawn design in red, yellow, and green. Dated 1846, it comes from Jämtland. Shallower than the earlier ones, it was used to hold food and as a decoration near the hearth.

Right. Yellow, red green and brown are the colors used for this impressive little Bowl from the southern province of Skåne. It hung from the wall by one handle. When in use it held porridge.

Bowl designed by Gunnar Nylund for Rörstrands Porslinsfabriker, Lidköping. A famous piece which makes distinguished use of the crown motif in a translucent effect. White porcelain.

Above. Flintware by Gertrud Lönegren.

Right. Vase by C. H. Stålhane.

Below. Pottery pieces by Charlotte Hamilton.

All pieces executed for Rörstrand.

Above. Stoneware Teapot and china Cup by Gunnar Nylund for Rörstrand. *Left*. Two-spouted china Teapot, divided in two compartments to hold both tea and hot water. By Gunnar Nylund for Rörstrand.

Below. Double Teapot (hot water jug below) designed by Gunnar Nylund and decorated by Lis Lundquist. For Rörstrand.

Brown Glaze by Wilhelm Kåge for Gustavsberg.

Polychrome by Stig Lindberg for Gustavsberg.

Above. Earthenware Plate decorated by C. H. Stålhane.

Right. Peking Duck. Mat glaze. By Gunnar Nylund. Both for Rörstrand.

Polychrome by Stig Lindberg for
Gustavsberg.

Left. Brown-glazed Stoneware Bowl.

Right. Salt-glazed Stoneware.

Left. Earthenware Vase with scratched slip decoration.
All designed and made by Edgar Böckman, Stockholm.

Pottery and Tile designed
and made by Gocken Jobs.

All for NK:s Textile Workshop.

Vase, Pitcher, and Cup by Lisbet Jobs; Figurines
by Gocken Jobs. All for NK:s Textile Workshop.

Left. Glazed pottery Musicians by Lisbet Jobs, for NK:s Textile Workshop.

Below. Wall Plaque. Fishes in stoneware relief. Made by Tyra Lundgren. Fired at Gustavsberg.

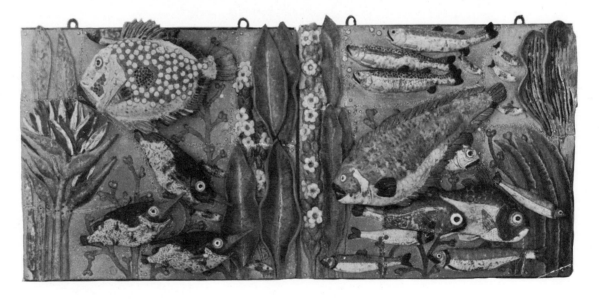

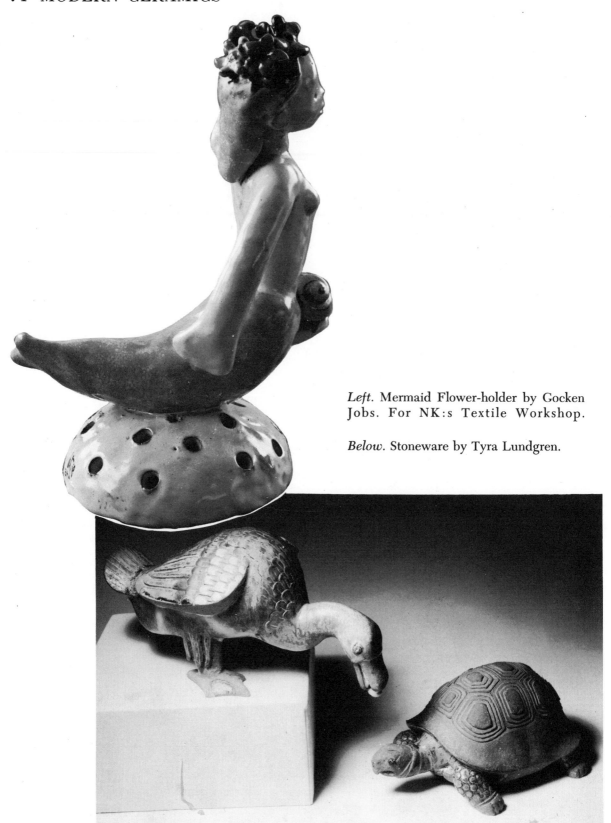

Left. Mermaid Flower-holder by Gocken Jobs. For NK:s Textile Workshop.

Below. Stoneware by Tyra Lundgren.

CHAPTER IV

METAL

IN recent years a complete set of smith's tools, dating from the 10th century was found on the island of Gotland, off the east coast of Sweden. The hammer and tongs, which had been stored in a chest for centuries, were much the same type as those used in Sweden today, and the general character of the tools indicated that carpentry and coppersmithing were a part of the craftsman's work during those early times. It is not surprising that many weapons, such as swords, spears, and arrow points, should have been preserved, since they were traditionally placed in graves along with fallen heroes, but it is surprising to know that many ornamental and useful things were forged of iron in those remote days. Locks, fittings, and iron household articles from the 9th and 10th centuries have been found on Birka, an island in Lake Mälar, the site of the first town of any consequence in Sweden. All these things are evidence of a high standard of skill in forging in ancient Sweden.

By the early part of the Swedish Middle Ages, the smiths were forging exquisite and highly decorative products. The iron-bound church doors of the 12th and 13th centuries are the most striking. Iron decoration was a combination of imported Roman patterns and native traditional, interlaced with dragon heads as well as human and animal figures. Similar motifs were used to decorate chests with iron mounts.

With the 14th century came a decline, and by the 15th century iron work had become less decorative almost to the point of being monotonous. But the growing importance of towns in Sweden in the 16th century created new needs for iron work. The work of the town craftsman increased in output and in importance. He belonged to a highly organized guild. The rural smith, however, had the right to carry on his work in the country independent of a guild, a right of which he made industrious use.

These craftsmen followed traditions of the Viking times and of the early Middle Ages. In the handwritten "landskapslagarna" of the 13th century, smiths are referred to as a class of rural craftsmen. Traditionary types of iron work came down through the centuries, and even as late as the 17th and 18th centuries locks of a type identical with those used in Viking times were still being made in Dalarna.

In his workshop in the village, the rural smith made simple objects for everyday use. He made all sorts of needed things, but sometimes a special item would be sold to surrounding districts, and as other smiths in other districts became known for their particular work, his own work would become more specialized. In this way a province gradually became known for a particular item. Dalarna became the scythe-making province; spikes were made in Närke, while Västergötland became known for fine knives. Highly skilled gunsmiths worked in many provinces.

By the second half of the 17th century it became easier to obtain plentiful supplies of iron of good quality. The industry grew, and the peasant smiths became prosperous and artistically ambitious. A characteristic of the rural smith was his fondness for pendants, usually in the form of leaves, symbolic of the Tree of Life. He hung these profusely on the iron grave crosses which were used in Sweden instead of stone markers. The crosses took on many shapes with local characteristics. The iron markers from Småland and Ostergötland were thick and heavy; in Värmland the crosses were large, with many arms, and in Västmanland the designs were even more complex. In Jämtland simple crosses with many rings were the custom. The initials, and dates pertaining to the deceased, were usually stamped into little iron weathervane flags at the top. The flags gave the crosses dignity, while the little leaf-shaped pendants which bangled in the wind gave the crosses an air that was anything but morbid.

Magnificent candlesticks were made on the anvil and were used for special occasions. On ordinary occasions the open hearth furnished light as well as heat, and less than a hundred years ago the peasant still obtained light from resinous wood torches placed in special holders on the wall. On holidays, however, tallow candles were burned. The candlesticks which held these were highly decorative affairs, sometimes designed as floor models, sometimes as chandeliers which hung from hooks in the ceiling and were adjustable. The shapes of these also had local characteristics, but rural smiths of all districts added rings and leafy pendants, and often the cock, symbol of light, was placed at the top of the candlestick. The cock has always played an important part in ancient Scandinavian religion. Old church belfries were never without the cock symbol.

In Scandinavia one finds the old and classical belief that fire was originally stolen by bold men from the gods; it was considered sacred, and, once kindled, was never allowed to go out. The fire which yields both warmth and light was indispensable in the cold northern climate of short days and long nights, and the very ancient dwellings were built as much to give shelter to the fire on the hearth as to give shelter to the people. The fireplace became of great importance in the preparation of food, and again the rural smith was called on to supply huge kettles in which to cook very thick porridge. He forged fire fans for grilling fish, and iron grills on which to cook elk steaks.

The work of the town craftsman had a character quite different from that of the rural smith. During the 16th and 17th centuries the town worker produced very free and fanciful patterns. The ornament and lattice work in gratings and grilles were twisted into playful loops; embellishments were in the form of grotesque human and animal figures. The iron worker's clients were the Royal Family, the nobility, and the well-to-do burghers in the still thinly populated towns. It was a fanciful style which made little impression on the rural smiths, though they did adopt a few locks and fittings. Once accepted, however, the embellishments became very popular, and their use has continued right up to the present time in Sweden.

In the middle of the 17th century Sweden came under the dominating influence of French art. From that time on the town smiths no longer worked out their own designs. With the new vogue in style, the smith had to confine himself to carrying out the wishes of the architect when the question of design arose. There was a conscious effort to conceal such things as locks, a disposition to regard them as a regrettable necessity.

The death blow to artistic blacksmith work came when cast iron was introduced during the later 18th and early 19th centuries. This technique was suitable for the time, with its new classic styles and with patterns borrowed from cast bronze work. But it never had the unique charm of the earlier forged iron.

A recent attempt to revive artistic wrought iron work began at the end of the 19th century, and during the present century it has achieved a lively appreciation as an independent art handicraft. This has been accomplished through the good work of the *Hemslöjd*. The Association commissions Swedish rural people of today to make candlesticks, hearth irons, and all the decorative household things produced by the former smiths. These are made after traditional designs furnished to the modern blacksmith by the *Hemslöjd* research department. The public has responded most favorably to the smith's output, thus encouraging him to the point of recreating many of the old traditional iron objects, which find their way into modern Swedish interiors, where they blend happily because of their honest lines, and create a highly decorative note.

ORNAMENTS

As late as 1850 a Swedish peasant woman was not considered properly dressed for a great holiday unless she wore a number of highly decorated silver ornaments. She was not allowed to wear such finery before she became a bride, but as a married woman she could don her great store of ornaments on special occasions, such as church festivals, weddings, and christenings. She had no trouble deciding which pieces she would wear—she simply wore all of them. Her rings, necklaces, and hanging buttons were purely ornamental. But some of the ornaments had a useful purpose. Her buckles, clasps, belts, pins and lacing stays were originally functional, and while they retained their purpose down through the years, they became more and more decorative until they finally became principally ornamental.

Probably the pendant worn around the neck is the most ancient type of ornament. It was an honored decoration everywhere among primitive peoples, and in Sweden there is an unbroken link between the prehistoric "*brakteater*" and the round, suspended ornaments worn by the later northern peasants. Forms and decoration of the hanging ornaments varied with time, but certain features survived. When Christian symbols came into use with the introduction of Christianity they were simply added to the already existing forms.

The hanging ornament was fastened to a very long chain which went around the neck many times, or to a number of shorter chains, each of which was fastened to the ornament. Occasionally a ribbon was substituted for the chain. The ornament sometimes took the form of a T, indicating a connection with the hammer of the god Tor. The Christian monogram A M (*Ave Maria*) was hung from it, as were also cup-shaped bangles. Rectangular silver plates and lockets were nearly as popular as medals and coins, either real or imitation. In any case there were always many hanging pendants, in various sizes.

The ring worn as a decoration on the finger is also a very ancient custom, an indication of wealth rather than a symbol of betrothal. In olden times the most important and binding part of the betrothal was the ceremonial presentation of gifts from the groom to the bride and her parents, a custom deriving from the primitive signification of buying the bride. These gifts generally included ornaments, especially rings, bought at the market fair in the nearest town. The modern Swedish custom of exchanging rings, whereby the bridegroom also receives a ring from his fiancée, did not become established with the peasants until the latter part of the 19th century. Up to comparatively recent

times, medieval characteristics still survived in the silver rings, such as hanging pendants and many small rings attached to the ring itself.

One of the ancient methods of fastening clothing was to push a wooden or bone needle through the garment. Once the art of working metals had been learned, however, the needle was made of silver and its efficiency was increased by combining it with a ring. And thus was invented the clasp, which was actually a decorative pin, since the needle went through the material of the garment. The pins worn by the peasant women fastened the chemise at the neck or were used to hold an embroidered kerchief together; they were either round or heart-shaped. The round ones were prehistoric in character; the heart-shaped ones were medieval in type and had many rhombic or cup-shaped bangles, usually engraved. The hearts were, in most cases, topped with a crown.

As far back as the Middle Ages, garments were held together by lacing through holes in the material or by lacing through rings sewed to the edge of the garment. These "*maljor*" were chiefly used for lacing the bodice which was attached to the skirt, and were so designed that when sewed to the garment an "eye" could extend over the edge and through this a ribbon or chain could be laced. The lacing was provided with a heavy engraved needle which was thrust in the bodice after it was laced up. Extra chain was left dangling over the breast. The lacing rings had local characteristics. Elaborate silver ones were fashioned in Skåne, while in Dalarna the rings were cast and made of pewter. Styles changed with the times. The medieval lacing rings were small, with human figures, angels, and animals, not too elaborately worked. With the Renaissance, which demanded tightly fitting garments, the *maljor* became more elaborate, with winged angel-heads and eagles with outspread wings. Occasionally pendants were hung to these, as with all other ornaments. During the 18th and 19th centuries the rings took on an exaggerated size, with schematized ornament and sets of cut pieces of glass.

There was no need for the gown-like clothes of the Middle Ages to be either buttoned, laced, or hooked together. But it was necessary to fasten together the cloak, which hung from the shoulders, with a hook and eye, and this finally developed into the richly ornamented cloak buckles of that period. Later the buckles were used on jerkins, which came into vogue during the Renaissance. The buckles were usually round, and all the motifs and bangles common to other ornaments were used on these too. In fact, they were often made to match some other piece. A red ribbon ruffle was usually sewed to the garment and the buckle was fastened to this.

Functional buttons did not come into general use among the peasants until the 18th century, but large decorative hanging buttons had been in use for a long time. Purely ornamental, they were attached to the jerkin at the shoulder or elbow, where they dangled prettily. Extra little bangles were often attached to the bottom of the button, making them even more effective.

Since the ancient gown-like clothes did not fit snugly to the body, a band was tied around the waist to make the garments warmer. This waistband came to be considered an essential part of the clothing, and even in prehistoric times the ends of the band were fastened so as to form a belt. The bands were either simple, woven affairs or were made of leather, often with silver mountings. Some of these mountings have been preserved from the Völkerwanderung Age (6th to 8th centuries), and belts made of silver plates are mentioned in the Icelandic sagas. In the 14th and 15th centuries, the dress of fashion had belts with big, square silver mountings. By the 16th and 17th centuries, narrow belts with thin mountings, or belts made only of metal plates attached to each other, were in vogue. The later Swedish peasant women retained the belt for a long time, at first with their everyday clothes and finally only as a part of their festive attire. From this use the "brudbälte" (bridal belt) arose, gradually becoming another one of the many gifts the bridegroom was expected to present to his bride. These were magnificent, of silver or of leather covered with red cloth with many silver mounts, usually with two small cup-shaped pendants hanging from each mount. Often chains that ended in silver balls or medals were hung from the earlier belts; in a later phase the groom, no doubt with an eye to the future, became more practical, and, instead of hanging ornaments, he attached to his bride's belt small leather-encased sewing implements. Gradually all these small hanging ornaments, useful and otherwise, were combined into one large decoration made of the same red cloth as that which covered the leather belt. Many silver plates were sewed to this in a double row, and it ended in one large silver ornament with more hanging bangles.

The "la," a headband worn by unmarried women, dates from prehistoric times. During medieval times it became an embroidered band or one made of red cloth hung with many silver bangles. It too became part of the bridal trousseau and was worn by the bride and her bridesmaids. Even when the bridal crown came into fashion during the Middle Ages the la was often worn along with the crown.

Since a crown was the special attribute of the Holy Virgin, the bridal crown became a symbol of virginity. In the old Swedish pagan rites associated with marriage, the wedding had been considered legalized by a ceremonial exchange of gifts and not by the religious ceremony. The clergy, therefore, strove to make the ceremony itself the factor that rendered the marriage valid, and one of the means was the regulation that the bride should be allowed to wear the crown of virginity only if she deserved to wear such a symbol; if she did not, her right to it was ignominiously denied. By a synod decision in 1584 it was determined that the churches should melt down the silver pieces which were not being used and of them make crowns to rent out to brides. As church property, these bridal crowns were costly affairs. The oldest crowns were very large and heavy, and fitted down around the head. In the 17th and 18th centuries they became smaller and were worn high on the head. In the late Renaissance period they became most elaborate, with hanging hearts and leaves and winged angel-heads riveted to the top ring of the crown.

Because the peasants were too conservative to discard any old forms of ornaments but simply added the more recent creations to the old, the number of ornaments worn by an 18th-century bride was appalling. Besides the la headband and her heavy crown she wore the large neck ornament, tied around her throat with a ribbon. In addition to this she usually wore two hanging neck ornaments, the long chain going around her neck many times. One was the gift of the groom, the other a gift from her parents. The hanging ornaments were fastened to either side of her bodice, so that the chains formed a draped pattern over the breast. Her bodice was tightly laced with a chain run through twelve silver lacing-rings, with the chain's needle tucked in her bodice along with two spoons. (The spoons would be used at the wedding feast, one for her and one for the groom.) Undergarments beneath the bodice were held fast with silver clasps.

Her kerchief was fastened with a larger, heart-shaped clasp. Her ring might be worn on her finger, or on one of the neck chains, or tied into one corner of her kerchief, depending on the custom of the province in which she lived. Large silver buttons hung at her elbows and from the shoulders. The wide red belt with many silver mountings which completed her adornment was next in importance to the crown on her head.

Many legends tell of brides collapsing beneath this burdening wealth of ornaments. In some provinces, according to custom, the bride was expected to run from her home to the church, and it is related that she often arrived at the church in a state of exhaustion.

For the most part the ornaments were made of silver, although in some few provinces they were brass or pewter. If pewter was the metal it was highly polished, and, like silver, was hall-marked to show the town where the ornament had been made, and the maker. Gilt came into use about the middle of the 18th century, and thereafter silver ornaments often were wholly or partially gilded. During the latter part of the 18th century the peasant silver underwent a considerable distortion of quality and its character became degenerated. In the province of Skåne, where the store of ornaments was larger and richer than anywhere else in Sweden, a tremendous exaggeration of form devel-oped during the 19th century. The ornaments were studded with imitation stones, and from a technical point of view the quality deteriorated when casting and pressing came into use. After about 1850, when the peasant dress customs began to break up, the ornaments lost their connection with dress and the general conception of elegance changed.

The modern Swedish smiths once more have taken up the hammer, and a strikingly high standard is seen in their present production, especially in silver pieces. There are many independently working silversmiths, and, as in all cases in Sweden, the large firms have endeavored to raise the level of their output by working closely with these artists. The combination of a feeling for the possibilities of the metals and technical skill has produced work of really distinguished quality.

Since 1920 a number of Swedish smiths have devoted their skill to bringing out the characteristic qualities of pewter. A temptation to try to give it the appearance of silver has been resisted, and the resulting heavy, dull-surfaced objects are unpretentious and worthy of high regard.

Whether they are done in pewter or in precious metals, the products of today have sound originality and always reveal the smith's identity. Often the creators are traditionalists; other smiths maintain a strict simplicity, but all of them produce pieces with much dignity of form.

12th-century wooden Door, with wrought iron mounts, from Rogslösa Church, Östergötland. At top a lively hunting scene is depicted. A hunter blows his horn to attract an unsuspecting reindeer, busily nibbling a leaf. Game drops from above, while the hounds run with great animation. The hinge below extends the entire width of the arched door. Rings fastened to a band of knobs over the hinge give it a special character. The rings are repeated in the elaborate door knocker. One large ring, the knocker, is suspended from a cuffed hand. When the large ring was banged against the encircling row of twelve smaller rings, each hanging from a knob, the resultant noise could be heard inside the church. Another band of rings on the outside of these was purely ornamental. The door has a lock and below it a handle. To the left of the handle is a small figure of a woman, who is awaiting the return of her hero, off fighting dragons. In battle armor and shield, with two guardian angels on either side of him, he stands over his kill, a two-headed dragon. In the lower left corner is the Tree-of-Life with the serpent on the ground. Above the serpent a bearded man subdues a woman; he grasps a club in one hand and her hair in the other. Above him she stands subdued, holding a small Tree-of-Life.

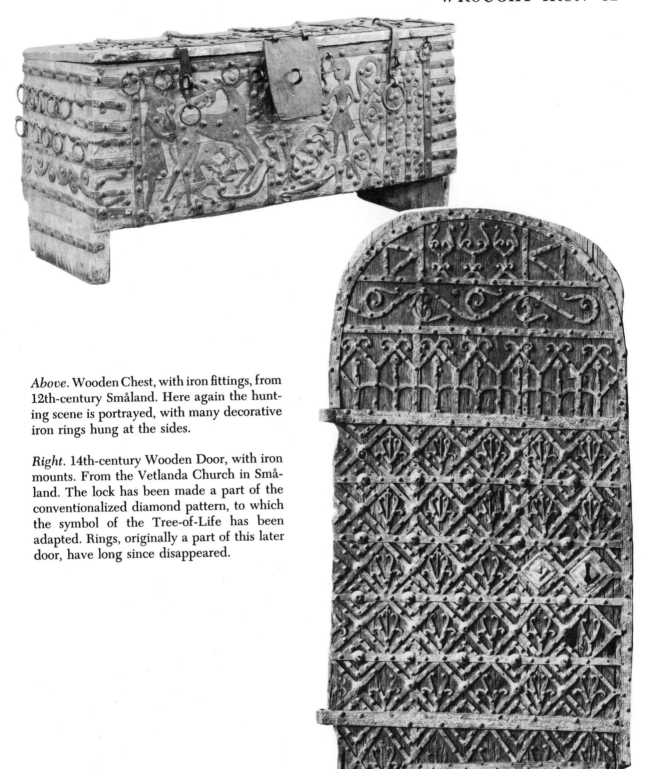

Above. Wooden Chest, with iron fittings, from 12th-century Småland. Here again the hunting scene is portrayed, with many decorative iron rings hung at the sides.

Right. 14th-century Wooden Door, with iron mounts. From the Vetlanda Church in Småland. The lock has been made a part of the conventionalized diamond pattern, to which the symbol of the Tree-of-Life has been adapted. Rings, originally a part of this later door, have long since disappeared.

Left. Padlock from the 9th century. It was found in a swamp on the island of Gotland, where it had been buried for centuries. Modern padlocks closely resemble this old Scandinavian lock made over a thousand years ago.

16th-century type Padlock.

Padlock, dated 1663, from the parish storehouse of the Little Mellösa parish in Södermanland.

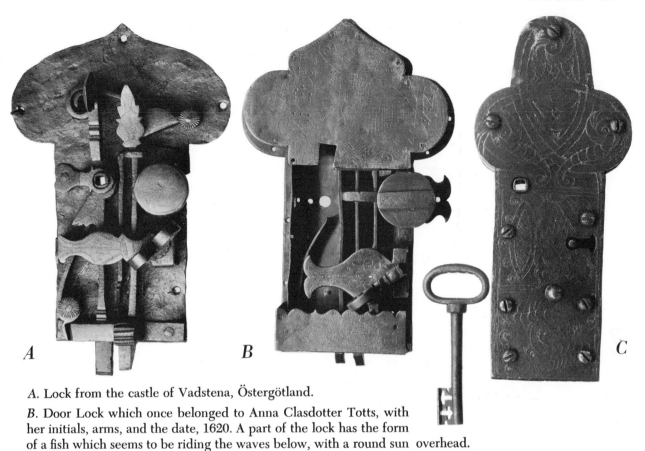

A. Lock from the castle of Vadstena, Östergötland.

B. Door Lock which once belonged to Anna Clasdotter Totts, with her initials, arms, and the date, 1620. A part of the lock has the form of a fish which seems to be riding the waves below, with a round sun overhead.

C. Door Lock, dated 1627, with arms of Gabriel Bengtsson Oxenstierna and Anna Gustavsdotter Baner.

D. Exposed mechanism of 16th-century Medieval-type Lock for a chest.

E. Padlock from the Fläckebo Church in Västmanland. Dated 1787, but of 17th-century type.

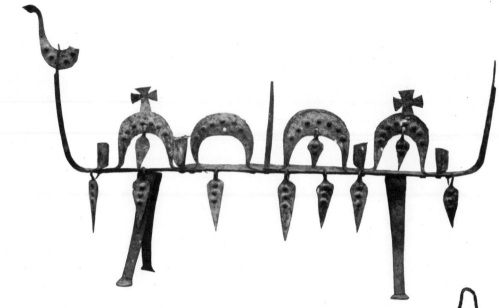

Wrought-iron "boat" Candelabra from the old church of Kyrkås, Jämtland. About 1500.

Above. Candlestick made from the ring of a chandelier of the Middle Ages. From Norrby Church, in Uppland.

Right. Medieval-type adjustable Chandelier, which hung from a hook in the ceiling of the Malung Church in Dalarna. The cock motif is a symbol of light.

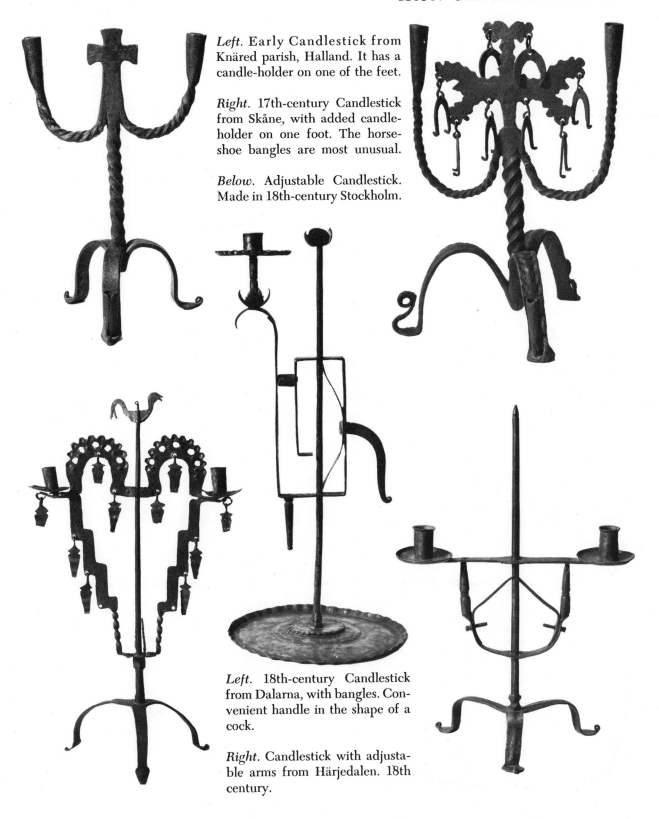

Left. Early Candlestick from Knäred parish, Halland. It has a candle-holder on one of the feet.

Right. 17th-century Candlestick from Skåne, with added candle-holder on one foot. The horse-shoe bangles are most unusual.

Below. Adjustable Candlestick. Made in 18th-century Stockholm.

Left. 18th-century Candlestick from Dalarna, with bangles. Convenient handle in the shape of a cock.

Right. Candlestick with adjustable arms from Härjedalen. 18th century.

Left. Grave Marker. From the Ekeby churchyard, in Östergötland.

Right. Grave Marker from Ukna churchyard in Småland, with dragon head "flag." 1829.

Right. Fine wrought-iron Cross with two small flags which turn in the wind, and hanging pendants. 1792. From Odensåker churchyard, Västergötland.

Right. Early Memorial Cross from the Mattmar churchyard in Jämtland.

Left. More elaborate iron Grave Cross using the same symbolic sun motif. From the Västerfärnebo churchyard in Västmanland.

Above. Sign from a tavern in Stockholm. The arm with upright lily and tulip was made in 1600. A hundred years later the original pendant sign was replaced by that of the "Central Tavern." A wreath of wrought-iron bunches of grapes further emphasized the tavern's wares.

Below. The upper part of a window from a 17th-century building in Stockholm.

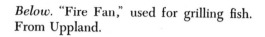

Below. "Fire Fan," used for grilling fish. From Uppland.

Above. Openwork iron Window Grille from the castle of Vadstena, in Östergötland. Made in 1500.

Iron Grill used for grilling meat. From Värmland.

Above. Iron Candlestick using the traditional cock motif, symbol of light. Made especially for the Hemsloyd in Stockholm.

Above, right. Firedog made for the Hemsloyd of Upsala.

Right. Firescreen, modern. Designed by Per Ingvarsson and forged by Robert Nilsson.

Above. Crosses which hung from chains were not the four-armed Latin crosses. The Swedish ornamental crosses consisted of only three arms and probably had some connection with the hammer of the god Tor, frequently used as an ornament and amulet in Swedish prehistoric times. At the same time, they had appendant Christian symbols, such as the Ave Maria monogram, according to Medieval custom.

Left. A medal, coin, or imitation of either was often worn from a chain, frequently two and one half yards long, which went around the neck many times. A thin, twisted rod surrounded the medal or coin and to it an uneven number of cup-shaped bangles were fastened, usually three or·five, and sometimes in varying sizes.

Right. Hanging Medal Ornament from Skåne. On the side shown is the likeness of Queen Christina. Gold plated on silver, a trend that began about the middle of the 18th century.

Right. The silver "Locket-Chain" was the most favored neck ornament. Many chains were attached to either side of a rectangular locket. It was usually a bride's ornament and, if so, the heart motif was used with a small heart strung on a separate chain suspended from the locket. This one is gold plated on silver and comes from Småland.

Left. The Neck Ornament worn just under the chin is of a later type. A silk ribbon was strung to clamps on the back of the rectangular part and tied around the neck. At the bottom of the rectangular piece, a pendant was hung by a ring with the letters IHS (Iesus Hominum Salvator). This ornament once had 23 dangling pendants of four different patterns and sizes. Made during the 19th century, when casting and pressing came into use to replace the more time-consuming methods followed in the earlier pieces.

Rings, like peasant ornaments in general, have kept their traditional old forms and ornamentation. Of these rings, shown oversize to bring out the detail, a number are purely
Medieval forms, although some of them were made as late as the 19th century. The hanging ornament in the form of the letters A M (Ave Maria) is a Catholic symbol which has
lived on among the peasants in spite of Reformation and Lutheranism. "Post-buttons,"
shown in each corner at bottom, were used to close the shirt neck-opening and were actually elaborate collar buttons. The left one is silver filigree; the right one is set with glass
"jewels."

"Hanging-buttons" in the pure Medieval tradition were wholly ornamental. They were fastened to the jacket at the elbow or at the shoulders. The later forms sometimes were put together in pairs and worn as cuff links or neck studs. Most of them are silver and come from Skåne. The 19th-century buttons often had colored glass sets, while the earlier ones were made entirely of silver. Also shown here are several examples of "post-buttons," described on the facing page.

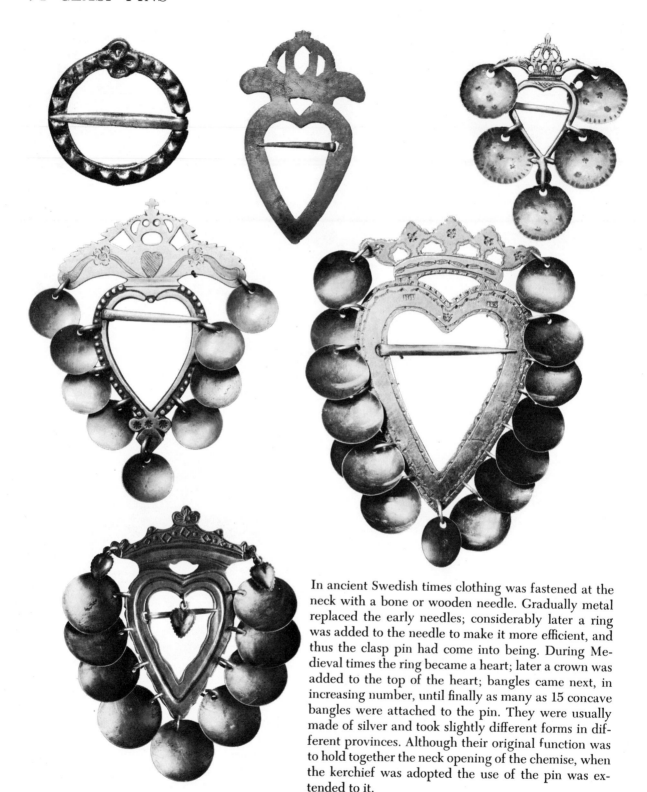

In ancient Swedish times clothing was fastened at the neck with a bone or wooden needle. Gradually metal replaced the early needles; considerably later a ring was added to the needle to make it more efficient, and thus the clasp pin had come into being. During Medieval times the ring became a heart; later a crown was added to the top of the heart; bangles came next, in increasing number, until finally as many as 15 concave bangles were attached to the pin. They were usually made of silver and took slightly different forms in different provinces. Although their original function was to hold together the neck opening of the chemise, when the kerchief was adopted the use of the pin was extended to it.

"Maljor" were lacing-rings which were attached to the bodice. Through these a ribbon or chain was threaded to hold the garment together. A heavy metal needle was fastened to the end of the ribbon or chain in order to facilitate the lacing. When the bodice was pulled tightly together, the needle would be thrust into the top of the bodice, with a part of its ornate end showing. Maljor are connected with the dress of the late Middle Ages and the Renaissance, which demanded tightly fitting garments. The rings were usually executed with some sort of decoration, the most elaborate coming from Skåne. The rings reproduced here have been slightly enlarged. The winged angel-head at the left and the Ave Maria monogram (above, center) have Renaissance character. Many of the rings from Skåne have retained a Medieval character. The three below, right, are of Medieval type. The others show by their exaggerated sizes, their schematized ornamentation, and inlays of colored glass, that they are of a much later type, from the 18th and 19th centuries. The engraved brass needle (in enlarged size) to which the lacing chain was attached comes from Fjäre, Halland.

The silver lacing-rings shown in the column of pairs at the far left are of the Medieval and Renaissance type, in which the eye is incorporated in the design as a part of the ring itself. In the three pairs above and at left, which are from Dalarna and are cast and made of pewter in a great variety of patterns, the eye is a distinct part.

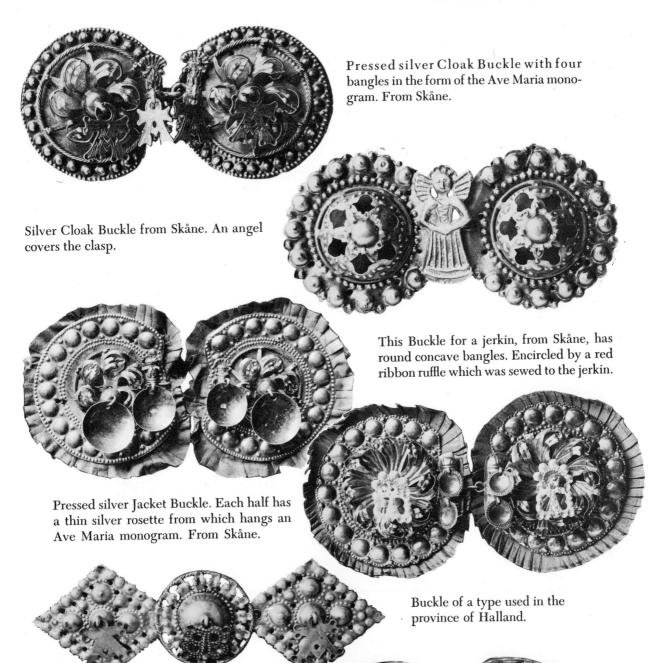

Pressed silver Cloak Buckle with four bangles in the form of the Ave Maria monogram. From Skåne.

Silver Cloak Buckle from Skåne. An angel covers the clasp.

This Buckle for a jerkin, from Skåne, has round concave bangles. Encircled by a red ribbon ruffle which was sewed to the jerkin.

Pressed silver Jacket Buckle. Each half has a thin silver rosette from which hangs an Ave Maria monogram. From Skåne.

Buckle of a type used in the province of Halland.

Later type 19th-century Buckle from rural Skåne, studded with bits of colored glass. Inspired by jewels of the upper classes.

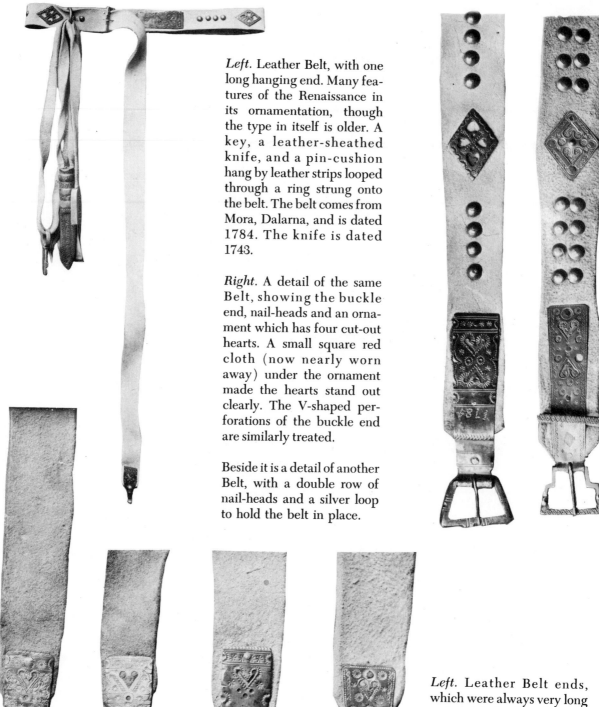

Left. Leather Belt, with one long hanging end. Many features of the Renaissance in its ornamentation, though the type in itself is older. A key, a leather-sheathed knife, and a pin-cushion hang by leather strips looped through a ring strung onto the belt. The belt comes from Mora, Dalarna, and is dated 1784. The knife is dated 1743.

Right. A detail of the same Belt, showing the buckle end, nail-heads and an ornament which has four cut-out hearts. A small square red cloth (now nearly worn away) under the ornament made the hearts stand out clearly. The V-shaped perforations of the buckle end are similarly treated.

Beside it is a detail of another Belt, with a double row of nail-heads and a silver loop to hold the belt in place.

Left. Leather Belt ends, which were always very long and finished off with a silver ornament. The design matched that of the buckle end.

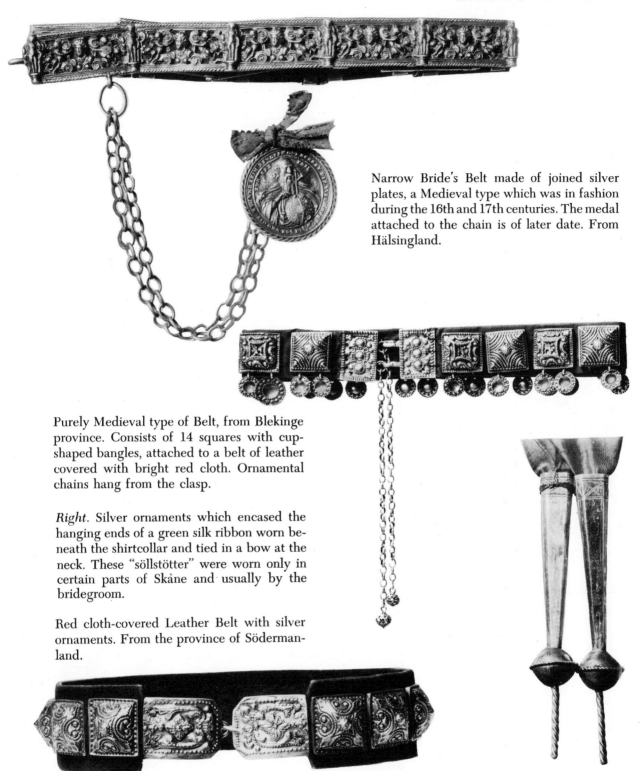

Narrow Bride's Belt made of joined silver plates, a Medieval type which was in fashion during the 16th and 17th centuries. The medal attached to the chain is of later date. From Hälsingland.

Purely Medieval type of Belt, from Blekinge province. Consists of 14 squares with cup-shaped bangles, attached to a belt of leather covered with bright red cloth. Ornamental chains hang from the clasp.

Right. Silver ornaments which encased the hanging ends of a green silk ribbon worn beneath the shirtcollar and tied in a bow at the neck. These "söllstötter" were worn only in certain parts of Skåne and usually by the bridegroom.

Red cloth-covered Leather Belt with silver ornaments. From the province of Södermanland.

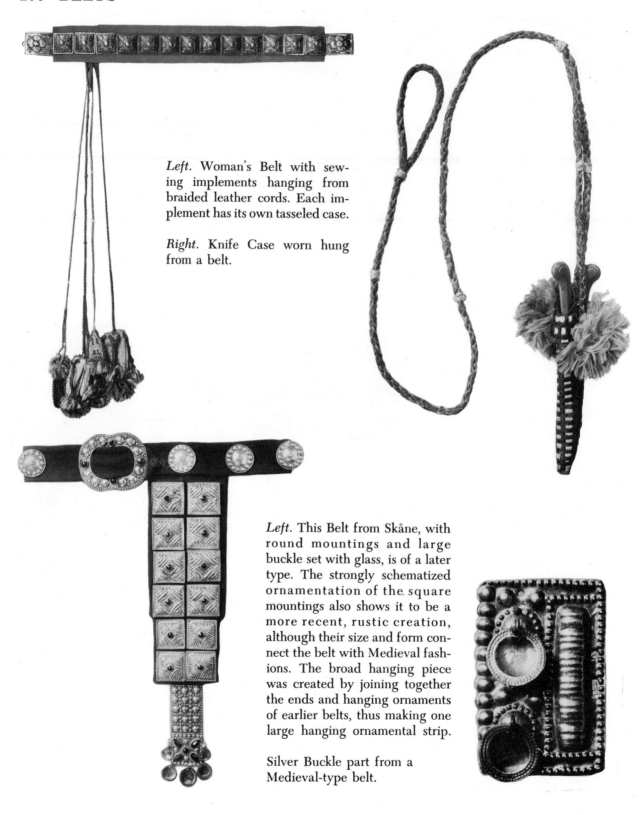

Left. Woman's Belt with sewing implements hanging from braided leather cords. Each implement has its own tasseled case.

Right. Knife Case worn hung from a belt.

Left. This Belt from Skåne, with round mountings and large buckle set with glass, is of a later type. The strongly schematized ornamentation of the square mountings also shows it to be a more recent, rustic creation, although their size and form connect the belt with Medieval fashions. The broad hanging piece was created by joining together the ends and hanging ornaments of earlier belts, thus making one large hanging ornamental strip.

Silver Buckle part from a Medieval-type belt.

Bridal Crown from Södermanland, made during the early 18th century. The points with hanging leaves and ornaments riveted to the crown ring are typical of the late Renaissance.

A bride sometimes wore a Chaplet or "*La,*" instead of or with the crown. It was either an embroidered band or made of cloth with silver ornaments, and was an older type of head ornament than the crown. The top Chaplet is a Medieval type made of red cloth with hanging engraved leaves. The lower band, also made of red cloth, has the Medieval type of silver fittings. The hanging coins have the effigy of King Karl XIV and have round cup-shaped bangles fastened to them. Both are from Skåne.

Above. Modern adaptation of the traditional Bridal Crown. On the very top is a tiny church with moonstone windows; it is supported by two crossed silver bands which represent the Cross. Pendant angels (shown in detail at right) make heavenly music. The crown is set with pearls for chastity and with aquamarines for life and hope. The Blood of Christ is symbolized by rubies set in the rim of the crown, which is small and rests on top of the head.

Below, right. Fanciful silver Cup set with amethysts.

Below. Silver Coffee Service. Ebony handle and knob.

All by Jacob Ängman for Guldsmeds Aktiebolaget, Stockholm.

Above, left. Silver Cup, wholly hand-made of one piece of silver, with festoons of gold, and set with 72 real stones, among them diamonds, emeralds, and rubies.

Above, right. Silver Cigarette Container, silver Cigarette Tray, and silver Water Pitcher in unusual triangular shape with silver and ebony handle.

All designed by Helge Lindgren and made by K. Anderson, Hofjuvelerare (Jeweler to the King).

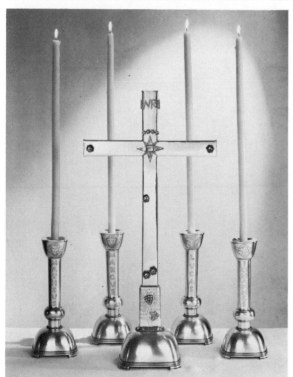

Left. Church Silver designed and executed by Sven-Arne Gillgren for Guldsmeds Aktiebolaget, Stockholm. The Cross is set with symbolic stones. Each of the four candlesticks has, engraved on its drop-cup, a motif symbolic of one of the four evangelists, Matthew, Mark, Luke, and John.

Above, left. Gold Cup with engraved leaf design.

Above, right. Silver Candlesticks.

Left. "Spring," engraved silver Cup, with enamel flowers.

All designed and executed by Sven-Arne Gillgren for Guldsmeds Aktiebolaget, Stockholm.

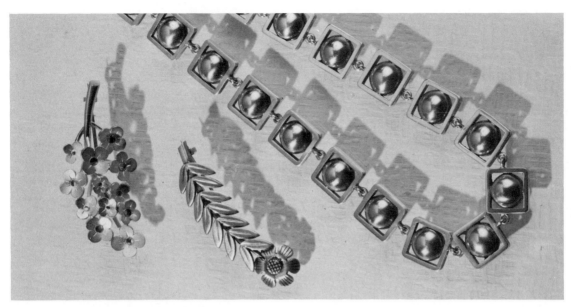

Above. Hand-made Necklace and Pins.

Below. Cigarette Boxes with flower knob-handles.

All designed by Erik Fleming for Atelier Borgila, Stockholm.

Below. Hand-made pewter Jewel Box, designed by Estrid Ericson for Svenskt Tenn.

Left. Polished brass Candlestick with glass drop-cups. Designed by Joseph Frank for Svenskt Tenn.

Left. Gold Bracelet designed by Sigurd Persson. Each link symbolizes one of the Arts.

Below. Polished pewter tea Service with wood handles and knobs. By Joseph Frank for Svenskt Tenn.

CHAPTER V

GLASS

SWEDEN'S international reputation for fine glass is no mere accident.

With the advent of industrialism, Sweden, like all countries, suffered a debasement in taste. In the lurch from decorative blown glass to that of industrial manufacture, the standards of design and quality were required to change too rapidly. This condition was recognized, and under the sponsorship of the state-aided organization, *Svenska Slöjdföreningen,* glass factories began employing artists as designers and production leaders. The result of this close cooperation was a great improvement in the esthetic as well as the technical quality of glass.

Kosta, established in 1742, is the oldest glass works in Sweden among those in operation today. When the new movement to improve the manufacture of glass began in 1917, Kosta was one of the pioneers in engaging artists to design glass that would bring out the character of the material to best advantage, at the same time producing objects suited to their function and generally acceptable to the public.

Orrefors, founded in 1897, also realized the need of artistic direction when in 1916 they began producing art glass. Two of Sweden's outstanding artists, Edward Hald and Simon Gate, were called in to design and decorate Orrefors glass; later another artist, Vicke Lindstrand, joined them. While each of the three artists had his own distinctive style, their combined efforts raised the output of Orrefors glass to a high artistic level. A unique Orrefors feature is the intaglio engraving of massed designs on the thick glass body of vases, bowls, and decanters.

The contrast between the smooth glass surface and the boldly engraved design produces a striking and rich effect.

The art of engraving glass is not new in Sweden. It was introduced into the country by Anthony Seifferd, from Erfurt, who worked in Stockholm from 1650 to 1660. At about the same time Elias Horn came from Dresden and worked in Stockholm until his death in 1673. These two were masters, and with them they brought all the methods of work learned in their early years of professional training. They were commissioned to supply the Royal Palace in Stockholm with fine glass goblets and spirits-containers bearing the engraved monogram of Charles XI. Glass had been regularly produced in Sweden since 1556 and the engravers for the most part did their work on Swedish-made glass. Melchior Jung's glass-house in Stockholm supplied Seifferd and Horn with some of the glass they used, and other glass objects suitable for engraving were imported. The need for importing glass ceased, however, when the Kungsholm glass factory was established in 1679 and began producing glass of finer quality and greater quantity. Kungsholm proved to be a long-lived and profitable enterprise. From an economic point of view the 1760's were its best years, but from an artistic standpoint the years spanning the end of the 17th century and the early 18th century were its best.

The most important engraver at Kungsholm was Kristoffer Elstermann, who worked there from 1691 until he died in 1721. He was employed as the Court glass engraver, and his name appears many times in the account books of the Dowager Queen Hedvig Eleonora. A German by birth, Elstermann probably received his professional training at Nuremberg, for he introduced many motifs characteristic of Nuremberg glass engraving of that time, such as the crossed palm and laurel branches, small scattered flowers, the radiant-sun, and the lambrequin border. The laurel or palm sprays were crossed in such a way as to surround a monogram or some other central ornament, such as a coat-of-arms. On the opposite side or "back" of the glass, the radiant-sun motif was often engraved to balance the heavily engraved monogram. The five-pointed North Star motif was applied in the same way as the radiant-sun. The former, however, was strictly a national motif which had been introduced by Charles XI.

Typical of Kungsholm glass up until about 1725 are the surface-covering small scattered flowers, and flower motifs used for the purpose of filling. Landscapes and figures were rarely used as decorative material by the engravers. Simple wreaths of leaves formed early rim borders until Elstermann introduced the lambrequin and more elaborate flower borders. Contemporary and subsequent engravers adopted and continued Elstermann's ornamental style, although they never quite attained his perfection of design or of technique.

When cut glass became a vogue, the art of glass engraving began to be held in less esteem. The Kungsholm glass house commenced cutting glass in the decade of the 1730's, and the fact that the term "engraver" disappeared from the records of this and other glass-houses from about 1750 to 1800 is significant of the decline in the prestige of engraved glass. Glass-cutters are mentioned often in the old records, however. That the workers in glass practiced both methods of decoration is known.

Besides the dominating Kungsholm glass works, there was another house, established in 1691, the Skånska glass-house in the northern part of the province of Skåne. Work was carried on at Skånska until 1762, when the factory was completely destroyed by fire. Skånska, like Kungsholm, engraved objects which were on the whole associated with German forms. The patterns were the conventional ones of that period. Round bowls with lids were peculiar to Skånska, however, and small tumbler-like wine glasses were also typical of the house. It is the engraving, not the patterns, which characterizes Skånska glass. The house had no leading engraver, as did Kungsholm, and in trying to imitate the skilfully and dextrously executed designs of Kungsholm, Skånska fell short in technique. The palm leaves were much too thin and gave an impression of swaying, the laurel branches became twiggy and all but lost their identity. The difficulty entailed in trying to cope with the elaborate designs of other houses resulted in a more rustic and schematic engraving which still had a certain definite charm.

After the close of the great wars of Charles XII, many national industrial enterprises were founded, and glass-houses were among them. There were twelve 18th-century glass-houses established in Sweden besides the already existing Kungsholm and Skånska houses. Of these twelve, six produced engraved glass — Limmared, Kosta, Kasimirsborg, Göteborg, Strömbäck, and Cedersberg. Except at the Kosta house, no regular engravers were employed. Glass engravers wandered from one factory to another, staying long enough to engrave all the glass on hand and then moving on. In consequence, no glass was produced that was characteristic of any one house.

All the engraved decoration was markedly Baroque during the latter half of the 18th century. It is curious to note what small influence rococo had on engraved ornamentation. By the end of the century, neo-classicism had gained its foothold. But no matter what the style or type, Swedish engraved glass of the 18th century had a character all its own.

Modern Swedish glass has retained many of these characteristics, though changing with the styles of the times. The only influence the machine has had on glass is a general influence on the decorative motifs used and not on the actual process of manufacture. The ordinary ideas of mass production do not apply to glass making, for it still takes as much skill and imagination to create beautiful objects in glass as it did in the 18th century.

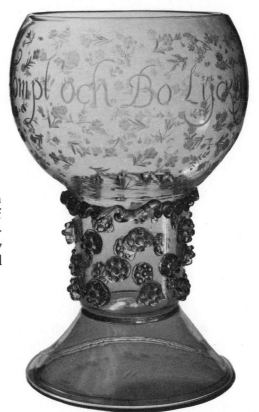

Right. Rummer made at the Kungsholm glass-house in Stockholm during the time of Kristoffer Elstermann. Characteristic of 18th-century Kungsholm glass is the hollow flattened ball stem and the engraved small scattered flowers. 1700-1720.

Left. Tumbler with engraved inscription: "As Heaven Wills." Made at Kungsholm. Dated 1741.

19th-century "Supglas" for wine.

Baptismal Bowl made at the Kosta
glass factory in 1821.

"Strålaflaska," or Radiant-Sun
Spirits Flask, from Gästrikland.

Mug with lid, made and engraved at Cedersberg glass factory. Dated 1824.

Left. Spirits Bottle engraved on four sides. From Östergötland.

Right. Bottle and Glass, from the province of Halland. Engraved branches surround the monogram of Gustav IV Adolf.

Blown glass Spirits Bottle with flowers and birds
painted in enamels. From Älvdal, Värmland.

Wine Glass with engraved inscription and small floral pattern.

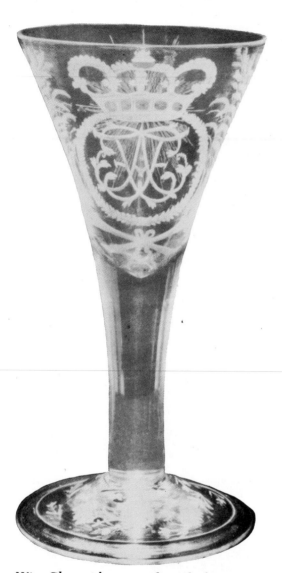

Wine Glass with engraved motifs characteristic of Kungsholm: crossed palm branches; laurel wreath topped with the royal crown; the radiant sun on the "back" of the glass, barely visible through the monogram of Adolf Fredrik; and small scattered flowers engraved on the foot.

Right. Wine Glass with small scattered flowers which nearly cover the surface.

All from Kungsholm glass-house.

Detail of a Drinking Cup showing the North Star motif engraved on the "back" of the glass. Laurel and palm sprays at the sides cross under a monogram on the "front" of the glass. The North Star with its characteristic five points is a strictly national motif.

Goblet made between the years 1720-1750. Engraved with floral borders and inscription.

Detail of a Drinking Cup showing the radiant sun engraved on the "back" of the glass.

All from Kungsholm glass-house.

18th-century engraved Kosta Decanter.

Glass Tankard with handle from the Skånska glass-house. Engraved inscription: Henrich Heller and Anna Lisa Loo.

All designed by Edward
Hald for Orrefors Glas-
bruk, Orrefors.

Above. Cut Graal glass Bowl.

Right. Hand-blown Vases with turned-over rims.
Pale violet.

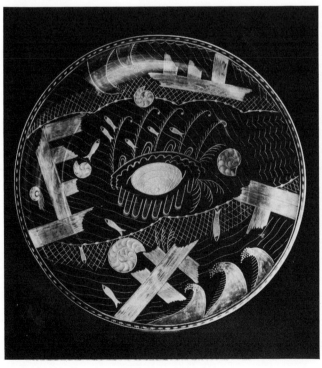

Left. Engraved Dish, "The Broken Bridge."

All designed by
Simon Gate for Orre-
fors.

Above. Engraved Platter.

Right. Graal glass Vases. The
taller one has blue and gray flowers and a dark blue rim.

Left. Graal glass Vase. Clear glass with motif in brown and red.

Right. "St. Francis and the Birds," engraved glass Vase.

Both by Vicke Lindstrand for Orrefors.

Clear glass with blue.

Yellow glass with dark green and red.

Clear glass with dark green.

Clear glass with black and brown.

All designed by Edvin Öhrström for Orrefors.

Left. "Mother and Child." Engraved glass Vase by Sven Palmqvist.

Right. "Cinderella." Engraved glass Vase by Nils Landberg.

Both for Orrefors.

Right. Cut glass Vases.

Below. Blown glass. Shaped while hot.

All by Elis Bergh
for Kosta Glasbruk, Kosta.

Left. Cut glass Vase, leaf design.

Below. Vase and Ashtrays, with pattern formed by acid-etching the overlay.

By Sven-Erik Skawonius for Kosta.

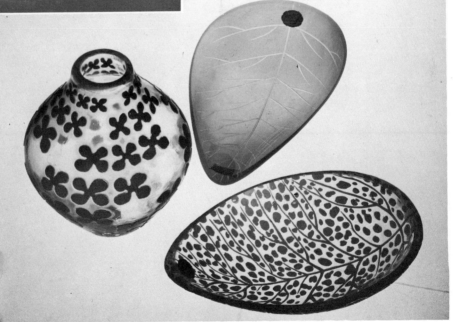

Left. Cut glass Vase and furnace-treated Bowl. By Edvin Ollers for Åfors Glasbruk, Emmaboda.

Right. Cut glass Vase, pale gray, designed by Gerda Strömberg for Strömbergshyttan, Hovmantorp.

CHAPTER VI

WOOD

IN THE old days the Swedish peasant house was built on a very simple plan: one large main room and a smaller storage room, with a hall separating the two.

The entrance door, so low and wide as to be almost square, led into the hall. On entering the house it was necessary to stoop in order to clear the low door frame; at the same time one needed to step high to avoid stumbling over the wide upright plank across the bottom of the entrance. The plank was a necessity during the long winter months, as it served to keep the heavy snow from drifting into the house when the door was opened. Wooden pegs lined the walls of the hall. Here the peasants could shed their snow-laden fur-skin jackets and leave their huge straw overboots.

A door led from the hall into the large main room, which was literally a living room. Here the housewife did the cooking for her family on the great fireplace, which had a built-in oven at one side. The fire was never allowed to go out from the time of the first frost until the spring thaw, and the coffee-pot on the hearth was as constant as the fire. The food was served on the long table by the window. All members of the family, which usually included in-laws, slept in built-in beds which lined the walls. If the household had servants, they too slept in this room. The children were given the upper beds. A step alongside the bed made climbing into it somewhat easier. The step also held the sleeper's shoes and the standing clock of which nearly every rural home could boast. An elevated recess between the brick wall of the fireplace and the outside wall provided space for another bed which was assigned to the oldest member of the family, or to one who was ill, as it was the warmest sleeping place in the room.

In this same room the man of the house carried on his trade or craft. If he was a clock-maker his tools and work-table would be beneath the low, small windows. If he was a wood craftsman, or a painter, his work-bench and materials were by the windows where the reflection from the snow afforded him better working light.

A wooden or leather cradle was suspended near the bed closest to the fireplace. Other hooks in the ceiling held the child's hanging-chair. The fact that there were several of these ceiling hooks made it possible for the mother to place her child by the warm fire, by the window, or wherever was convenient.

Hooks in the ceiling held two huge drying poles called "crown-rails," which had carved sides and dragon-head ends, their decoration being another example of the survival of Viking traditions. In olden days the rails had a unique function. They divided the room into three parts, the least distinguished section being nearest the door and the most important at the far end of the room. If a crime was committed in the house, the punishment was determined, not so much by the nature of the crime, as by the section in which it was committed. The severest punishment was dealt to the offender committing a crime in the most important section farthest from the door.

Unadorned poles around the top of the fireplace

held wet clothes, while other poles supported the winter's supply of hard bread, made in large, thin, flat cakes with an off-center hole in each, so that it could be slipped over the pole, there to hang until needed. It was made of a mixture of barley, oats, rye, and water, and baking took place once or twice yearly. The bread would keep indefinitely. In the old days it was the custom to have a special bread-baking when a girl child was born; the bread would be stored, and ceremoniously eaten on her wedding day.

The sturdy houses were built of great, heavy timbers. Rafters extended from the walls to the huge ridgepole at the top. On special occasions the rafters would be covered with painted, woven, or embroidered wall hangings, with a "ceiling dress" to cover the ridgepole.

From the hall a door opposite the main room led into the "*kistehuset*" (chest room), which was partly used as a spare bedroom, having a built-in bed in one corner. The room's main function, however, was to hold clothes and all the articles belonging to the household which were in evidence only on festival days. These articles were neatly stored in great wooden chests, each with its own special decoration, in which the date and the owner's initials were conspicuously painted as a part of the design. Each member of the family had an individual chest to hold his or her "church-going" clothes. If there were servants, they too had their clothes-chests in this room. Other chests held wall hangings and linens to be brought out for weddings, Christmas, and other occasions; still other chests held embroidered and woven cushions which at those happy times would be placed on all the benches and chairs. All these chests were lined up against the walls. Sometimes poles suspended from the ceiling took care of the overflow of linens if there were not enough chests to hold them.

In different parts of Sweden the peasant houses varied slightly from the generally typical arrangement of furniture and details of construction. In the far north the houses were usually ceiled, sometimes with a flat ceiling, sometimes following the slope of the rafters. The wall boards would often be painted in all-over patterns with an effect of wall paper as it is used today. The sloping ceiling boards usually had free designs painted on their whitewashed surfaces, while the walls had pictorial paintings. Wide floor boards were used throughout Sweden except in the very southern part, where floors were earthen. In some provinces small skylight windows in sloping ceilings were favored in preference to the usual small windows in the walls.

The furniture from central Dalarna seems particularly original, which is due in some degree to the fact that in this province traditional forms were preserved long after they had been abandoned in other provinces. However, the district around Siljan was one with a highly developed standard of craftsmanship in carpentry, and the furniture made there characterized the greater part of the whole province as well as neighboring districts. Angermanland was another province where the standard of craftsmanship was especially high, and during the 18th century carpenters in this province made magnificent cupboards, bedsteads, standing clock cases and small objects. A great deal of peasant furniture, splendidly painted in bright colors and richly carved, was produced in the northern Swedish provinces, the territory known as Norrland.

From records, we may assume that in ancient times social differences were not specially observed. In more recent centuries, however, this rather fundamental differentiation had a marked influence on peasant home furnishings. The furniture in homes of wealthy mine-owners and prosperous peasants differed not only in quality but in type from that in the modest households of land-renters and less prosperous peasants. Chests-of-drawers, tea tables, mirrors and wall clocks, for example, were to be found in the large peasant homes but were wholly lacking in the more humble dwellings. This situation began to change again during the 19th century, although social differences were still indicated by other pieces of furniture, such as the chiffonier.

The simpler pieces of furniture—chairs, boxes, wall shelves, and the like—were made by the peasants at home, but the larger objects were usually built by a local carpenter. The woods used were pine, spruce and birch. Still more imposing furniture could be bought at great fairs, and by the end of the 19th century, simultaneously with the disappearance of the local craftsmen, such pieces became quite common in peasant homes. These pieces of furniture did not, however, have a special peasant character, showing instead a more or less middle-class influence.

In ancient days, such furnishings as benches and beds were fixed to the walls, and even the tables were actually built into the house. During the 16th century, movable furniture began to appear, and

A chest room from Blekinge which was partly used as a guest room. All members of the household kept their personal belongings in individual chests. When not displayed, the wall paintings would be rolled and stored in one of the chests.

the types of furniture also changed, increasing in number. The chest, which had predominated for a long time, gave way to the cupboard. Chairs and settees took the place of long benches fixed to the wall. In the course of the 19th century, clocks and mirrors became more common among the peasants. With respect to form and decoration in general, the prevailing styles of a period were closely followed, since peasant culture very slowly adopted the new forms as they arose. Once accepted, however, they were held to with the conservatism that generally characterizes country people. Some forms which appeared to be new often were a transformation of an inherited style; this is especially true of the painted furniture from Dalarna.

The unique feature of the peasant home furnishings was the bedstead. In very early times the bedsteads were either simple benches constructed of heavy timber and fixed to the wall, or they were enclosed by shutters and called "closet-beds." If the built-in bedsteads had no shutters they were provided with heavy, homespun bed curtains. It was quite usual for two double beds to be placed end to end, and, in northern Sweden, one bed was often placed above another. Sometimes a bed had a cupboard at one end, and sometimes the lower bed had an extra sliding bed beneath it. These types were generally to be found all over Sweden,

with local variations as to form and as to placement in the room.

Although movable beds were never as popular as the built-in bedsteads, they did exist in some provinces at an early time. A mobile bed from Skåne is dated 1734, but is medieval in type, both as to construction and decoration, again showing the conservatism with which the peasants clung to traditional forms.

A characteristic type of bed for Sweden was the Gustavian bed, which had a high back and could be drawn out and lengthened. The backs were of many fanciful shapes with carved flowers and leaves, and sometimes were even adorned by carved fan shapes. These carvings were painted in many bright colors, and the beds themselves were usually painted white or blue, and, occasionally, red.

The peasants, always intrigued by the furnishings of the higher classes, often draped their beds with canopies of checkered homespun in the naïve belief that the result resembled the brocade drapes of the upper-class beds.

Since the Swedish peasant family was usually a large one and literally lived in one room of the house, it is not surprising that many pieces of furniture concealed beds which could be pulled out at night. A combination of table and bed was not

127

Interior of a less prosperous peasant household, showing four
beds. Ceiling poles hold the winter's supply of hard bread.

uncommon. Cupboards were often a combination
of bed and cupboard; the bed was underneath and
could be pulled out much the same as a drawer.

The *"dragsoffan,"* was, as the Swedish name suggests, a sofa that could be pulled out to make a
double bed. It was much like the Gustavian bed
except for a removable lid, which, when replaced,
made of it a sofa for daytime use. It was not until
the 19th century that sofas designed exclusively
for sitting upon became common. They were always built of wood in the style of the period.

An ancient type of mobile bench was the "turn-
over" bench, of medieval origin, which was widely
used in Sweden up to and during the early 18th
century. The back was attached to side posts of the
bench and had small knobs at the ends which fitted
into grooves in the legs. It was placed alongside
the dining table, and after the meal the back could
be turned over so that it faced the room, serving
then as a sitting bench.

Cupboards have always been prominent in rural
Swedish homes, dating back to the Middle Ages.
During the Renaissance and Baroque periods they
were as conspicuous a part of the furnishings as
the chest, finding especial favor in the well-to-do
southern districts. At a somewhat later date, richly
carved and ornamented cupboards appeared in the

northern provinces. The smaller three-sided cupboards were typical of northwestern Sweden.

The peasants often did their own decorating of
their painted cupboards; those with more elaborate
decoration were painted by artists who were even
better known for their wall paintings. On large wall
cupboards and sideboards dating from the 18th
century, the development from naturalistically
painted flower motifs to more conventionalized
decoration is to be observed.

A board laid across the knees served as a table
in ancient Swedish times. Later, the big plank was
placed on large blocks of wood, and after the meal,
it was hung on iron rings on the wall. The first type
of table made with under-framework was the trestle
table, which became the most common type in
peasant homes. The main table of the house, it was
used as the banquet table on feast days. Another
characteristically Swedish type of table was what
we know as the "sawbuck" table. The table was usually placed in one corner of the room near small
windows, in front of built-in benches which were
straw-filled and had woven covers.

In the far northern provinces, during the 17th
century the table tops were handsomely painted
with inscriptions, wreaths, and animals, whereas in
southern Sweden the table tops were usually left

Interior of a more prosperous peasant house in Dalarna in the beginning of the 19th century. "Bed-closets" with painted shutters, a sofa, cupboard, and clock, all painted, line the walls.

unpainted. In Skåne the wooden top was replaced by a stone top. Here, too, folding tables were quite common.

With the Renaissance, the familiar type of table appeared, with under-framework and four legs.

It was not until the end of the 19th century that the round table became common in peasant homes. Placed in the middle of the room, gradually it broke up the earlier scheme of furniture, in which items were ranged around the walls.

The main chair in the Swedish peasant home of old was not used as an ordinary chair or bench. It was regarded solemnly, as the seat of honor for an important guest, and when so used the chair seat would be covered with a cushion, embroidered or pattern-woven.

Characteristic of Blekinge province are the three-legged chairs with back joined into the seat. Probably the idea for these originated from the ancient stools which were made of a section of tree trunk, the legs being formed by the branches. If the natural branches were not enough to make a stool steady, an inset branch leg would be added.

Block chairs made of an entire hollowed-out section of tree trunk were used in northern Sweden in remote times. Other chair styles were the romanesque type, with turned uprights and horizontal

back pieces, and straw-bottomed chairs from Blekinge. In 1800 appeared the typically Swedish Gustavian chair, with straight back laths, a favorite style to this day.

The chest has had an important place in the lives of the peasants for many centuries. Even when the cupboard and the chest-of-drawers took over its functions, the chest did not disappear entirely; and it is only recently that the chest has finally come to the end of its career in Sweden.

The oldest chests had no lids, being constructed of four corner posts into which the sides were fitted. Chests of this kind from the early Middle Ages have been preserved, and one of the most remarkable dates back to the 12th century. Another ancient type, with rabbeted joints, dates from Viking times (800-1050). With both of these types, the ornamentation is of a very ancient style, with carved dragons and dragon heads.

The chest of more recent times had dove-tailed joints at the corners, and, in central Sweden, a flat lid. In southern and northern Sweden a convex lid was the rule. The art of furniture painting flourished luxuriously on these chests, and they are admirable examples of woodcarving.

Important too were the small painted boxes made to hold dress ornaments, bits of ribbon, and small

129

trinkets. The boxes from Södermanland are famous, as are those from western Sweden, which were often decorated with chip carving. The boxes from northern provinces, in common with furniture, show a strong rococo influence.

It was not until the 18th century that clocks began to appear in the farm houses, and then, naturally, in the larger ones first. At the beginning, the straight English-type clock styles were adopted, but toward the end of the century the rococo type with a circular face became common. In Sweden, these types are usually known as Dala or Mora clocks because the mechanism was manufactured in Mora, Dalarna, where this was a domestic craft. The clock cases vary not only with the changes of taste during the period but also with the degree of skill of the individual craftsman.

UTENSILS

A characteristic of Swedish peasant culture is the great variety of objects made of wood. In olden times the larger part of the domestic utensils used in the peasant homes were wooden. Judging from what has been preserved and from records, the craft of turning the lathe was commonly practiced during the Swedish Middle Ages (1050-1500). It is quite possible that the craft was known during the earlier Iron Age, although nothing has been preserved from that time. Only in very rare circumstances could prehistoric birchbark articles have withstood the onslaught of time.

In ancient times there were no plates, the people eating directly from the table top. Later, the food was served on a thin oblong board which was placed on the table for all to share. Finally it became customary for each one at table to have an individual board. The original large board was cut into pieces to make the smaller boards, and at first the pieces were cut square. Then corners were cut off, and finally the pieces were rounded. Thus the wooden plate came into existence.

Primitive bowls were made from natural outgrowths of trees, which were hollowed out, forming round or oval bowls. During the ensuing centuries these simple plates and bowls developed into all shapes and forms, and gradually carving and painting were added, until they became highly decorative articles.

As early as the 16th century it was necessary not only to serve a great abundance of food on the Swedish feast table, but also to put it before the guests in a creditable manner. Barley porridge, one of the principal dishes, was brought as a contribution gift by the guests in elegantly carved and painted wooden porridge-kegs. Contributions of food by the guests were essential, as marriages and other important events in a family, as well as festivals of the year, were celebrated among the peasants as a concern of the whole village. At a wedding or christening every guest was expected to take bread, butter, cheese or beer as a gift. The vessels in which these provisions were carried to the house of the feast were executed with scrupulous care, and the peasants vied in showing the finest basket, butter-box or porringer. The bread was brought in baskets made of elaborately latticed roots or woven chips, with painted decoration. Each guest was also expected to bring his own knife, fork, and spoon. Great pride was taken in these, especially the spoon. The handle of a spoon was always richly carved, and it was often a reminder of courtship days when the utensil had been given as a suitor's gift to his chosen one.

The food was placed on the table in large wooden vessels. Soup was served from a great bowl. Slabs of elk or reindeer meat, which was not everyday fare, were placed on wooden pedestal stands. Butter was sparingly used except at feasts, when it was

Below. Porringer with heart-shaped feet and burned ornamentation. From Småland.

consumed in incredible quantities and was dished up on a "butter stool" or "butter foot" of turned or carved wood, after being given a richer and more decorative character by the aid of a butter-press or butter-mold. Fish was served on wooden dishes with small hollowed-out sauce basins in the center, into which the fish could be dipped.

The meal would be topped off with tiny cakes. For these, each household had its own special cake stamps, which were round, square, diamond-shaped, or sometimes followed the shape of a carved design. Besides geometric patterns, birds, animals, hearts and even men on horseback were motifs used for the carving.

Although the Swedish country people ordinarily lived a most temperate life, on great feast days all restraint was laid aside. Ale was quite as important to the banquet table as food. It was fetched from the cellar in big hooped tankards with a spout for pouring the ale into smaller drinking vessels. In very early days, drinking vessels were actually bowls with four tips which served as handles; they were painted red, with a center sun motif and inscriptions. Some of the four-tipped bowls had a hole in the middle, with a rim around the hole; the ale was poured into the round trough between this rim and the rim of the outside edge. Such a bowl was aptly called a "keep-your-eye-open bowl," since a guest could keep a watchful eye on his neighbor as he raised the bowl to drink.

Other drinking bowls were deeper, with handles in the shape of the heads of animals and birds. It is not improbable that these were of prehistoric origin.

One of the most characteristic drinking vessels was the "ölgås" (beergoose), carved like a bird and painted, even to the red crest on the head. It floated on ale which was brought to the table in a great wooden bowl. From this bowl the guests helped themselves, dipping the "beergoose" into the liquid. When sometimes a stem in the shape of the fowl's feet was added, the "beergoose" stood on the table beside the bowl. These bird-shaped vessels were used mainly in the northern provinces.

Drinking customs differed in various parts of Sweden. In Uppland province it was the custom to bring the ale to the table in large tankards, from which it was poured into stoups with handles and lids, and richly ornamented with burned-in designs. The smaller tankards often had spouts, and the peasants drank the ale directly from the spout.

Each household had a wooden puzzle-cup. This was an ingenious affair. A guest was expected to drink from it, and if he could not guess the "puzzle" the contents would spill over him.

The peasant housewife used all sorts of wooden utensils in preparing a meal. Her decorative cake stamps and cheese molds were her pride and joy, but even the more useful things were never left unadorned. The flour she used was kept in a box with a carved or burned-in design. Often the box would have the shape of a bird, the head and tail being the handles, as in the drinking cups. An especially elaborate salt container hung on the wall by the hearth oven. A similar container held spoons, and was hung by the long dining table. A pear-shaped canteen was suspended by a leather strap near the door; it held milk and was used on long journeys through the woods. At berry-picking time the housewife used a special basket made of wooden strips woven around vertical staves, each of which ended in a decorative point. A similar basket hung at her loom to hold bobbins. It was her custom to carry a very thick porridge to any neighboring woman with a newborn child. Since she would meet there other friends bringing porridge, each woman took great pride in the keg which held the thick barley gruel. These wooden porringers were prettily decorated with carved, painted, or burned-in designs.

Boxes were an important item, as they not only held household and personal articles at home, but were carried on journeys, corresponding to our hand-bags and shopping-bags. The boxes were made on a large scale in all sizes and shapes, with simple or elaborate decorations by craftsmen, in the country as well as in the towns.

Boxes used for keeping articles of dress, such as gloves, caps, girdles, and the like, were larger and more ornate than those made to hold household items. These often have on them the initials of the owner, an inscription, and dates, as they usually were betrothal gifts. When the box was presented to the girl she found it filled with all sorts of carved things the young man had made for her.

Round boxes much like our hat-boxes held festive headgear. The "church-box" was carried by the women on Sunday and held the prayer book. Smaller boxes with snap-on lids were used for small articles, such as sewing materials, trinkets and ribbons. The man of the house kept his shaving equipment in a long box heavily decorated with chip carving. Another box held the seeds for spring sowing. In southern Sweden, each child had an individual *"barnäskorna,"* in which he or she was allowed to keep undisturbed any prized possession which had struck the childish fancy.

The ancient *"svep"* technique was used in the making of many types of boxes. Long, thin, flexible strips of wood were bent around a base and then fastened. The ends overlapped and were stitched together with birch roots. The woods used for *"svepta"* boxes were birch, oak, beech, spruce, or fir. The boxes were oval or round and usually had ingenious snap-on lids.

The decoration was burned, painted, or carved. Metal stamps, iron pins, and wheels made the burned designs in simple patterns of broken lines, or monotonously repeated patterns of dots, circles, half-circles, or S forms—all of them traditional and of prehistoric origin. The pattern styles changed down through the centuries until, by the 18th century, rich and elaborate plant forms were burned into the wood.

Painted *svepta* receptacles became the mode in Sweden during the latter part of the 18th century. The chief decorative characteristic was a naturalistic floral decoration, closely connected with the rococo style of ornament. The ground color was usually blue, with superimposed ornament in various colors, but generally in red and white, with a wealth of ornament around the monogram of the owner.

Another old type of decorating used in the northern provinces was an engraving done with a knife; then soot or lampblack was rubbed into the incised design, which was usually of a geometric character.

Carved ornament on *svepta* articles goes back to a very remote time in Scandinavia. In Jämtland province a type of geometrical ornament has existed without a break since prehistoric times. Not until the 18th century, when the tulip gained its ascendancy, did simple plant forms appear, and rococo styles began to pull down the ancient and inherited traditions. Another style of carved ornament echoes the Renaissance, with animal figures in rows and on borders, geometric motifs, interwoven double running ribbon patterns, and symbolic signs and marks.

The very early carving was a simple knife-scratching. Later, pointed and V-shaped instruments were employed to produce relief carving, and finally *"nagelsnitt,"* a repeat pattern resembling a row of finger nails. This carved type of ornamentation is much older than the burned or painted kind.

Many wooden vessels were made of staves arranged around a solid wooden base and held together by wooden hoops. Simple hollowed-out vessels were made and used long before these staved vessels, but the staved type did exist even in Viking times and probably long before that. Milk kegs, drinking vessels, cans with spouts and barrels, were made in this way. Carved, stamped and painted designs decorated them. The painted articles tended to have a strong rococo flavor, showing a preference for plant ornamentation. Others showed the influence of the painted furniture of Dalarna.

Basket-weaving was a craft which was pursued by the poor, the blind, the disabled, and aged, and often was their only means of livelihood. Since its social role was that of saving people from the poor-house, basket work never enjoyed great reputation amongst the peasants. Most baskets were made for practical purposes, except for those woven to hold food contributions taken to feasts. Simple baskets held fish, salt, roots, vegetables, etc. Very large and impressive straw baskets held grain; they are made and used in southern Blekinge today.

Baskets were woven or coiled from various lengths of twigs, roots, wooden strips, bast-fibre, or straw. Several strands of material were braided

Meat stand used on the banquet table.
From Halland. 1806.

and woven in such a way as to give an openwork pattern. Stitching the basic material as it was being built up spiral fashion from the bottom gave other baskets an embroidered appearance. Lattice work on the side of some baskets resulted in a zig-zag pattern. Each province favored a particular method of basket-making, giving the baskets a local character.

These basket techniques have been kept alive by the *Hemslöjd* Association. Today many rural people supplement their incomes by making such baskets during the long winter months. They also carve and whittle many useful or purely ornamental things. The Christmas decorations are especially fine. Many of them are meant to be hung at the windows, such as angels carved from blocks of wood, with tin wings added; Christmas doves with wing feathers made of the thinnest wood, suspended by an almost invisible wire; large stars and snowflakes elaborately cut from thin pieces of wood.

Sometimes these are given a stain but usually they are left in the natural light wood color. The useful objects are carved with equal care. Salad bowls of all sizes and shapes, fruit bowls, ladles and forks, candlesticks, and boxes, made after traditional patterns, are a few of the things the country people produce to be sold in *Hemslöjd* shops throughout Sweden.

The great inlaid doors in Sweden are a particularly impressive feature of the modern buildings. The doors are flat, with many grained woods worked into modern designs. Motifs sometimes depict the function of the building in which the door is hung; other designs are based on traditional legends. Inlaid floral designs of an almost realistic nature decorate tables, chests, and tall clocks. This technique is used for murals as well. Panels of relief carving also decorate walls, furniture, and small objects which combine form and functionalism and are at the same time esthetically impressive.

Main room of a peasant house from Mora, Dalarna. Literally a living room, it shows many of the furnishings described in the foregoing text, such as crown-rails, curtained beds, craftsman's work table, block chairs, hanging cradle, branch-stool, drying rails, and a Mora clock.

Left. 16th century Bed from the central province of Dalarna. It is made up with bedstraw and two fur skins. The occupants slept between the furs. The coverlet, with the fur side down and the skin side covered with homespun, is the precursor of the *rya* coverlets.

Right. A fine example of the late Renaissance style of bed, from the mining district in Dalarna. Dated 1693. Two shallow cupboards at the foot of the bed have hinged doors provided with locks and keys:

Left. The conservatism of the Swedish peasantry and its clinging to tradition are shown in this oak bedstead from Långaröd, Skåne. Purely Medieval in ornamentation and construction, it was made as late as 1734.

Right. Built-in Bedstead with doors. From Norrbotten. The panels are painted red and yellow, with bright-colored floral designs. The chest-of-drawers at the foot of the bed, with a small cupboard above, has a dark brown brush-stroke design painted on a lighter brown ground-color.

Left. "Gustavian" Bed from Ångermanland. About 1800. It could be drawn out and lengthened and was intended for two persons. In this type the high back took many shapes and often was elaborately carved and painted.

Right. 19th-century "Gustavian" Bedstead from Småland. Painted white, with green knobs.

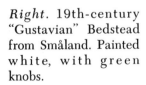

Above. Hanging Cradle from Dalarna with red, yellow, blue, and green painted design. A common type used in central Sweden, it hung by a leather strap fastened to a hook in the rafter. Several hooks in various parts of the ceiling provided a choice of places for hanging the cradle.

Right. Cradle with rockers parallel to the sides. From Norrbotten. Typical of the northern Swedish provinces. Made of carved pine and birch and painted in red, yellow, brown, and green. About 1800.

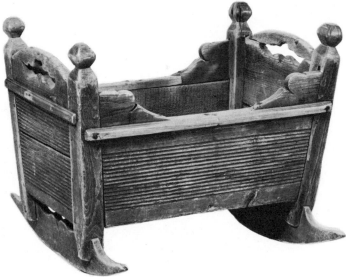

Left. A more common type of Cradle from Skåne, and typical of the southern provinces. It has rockers parallel to the ends of the cradle.

17th-century turn-over Bench from Hälsingland. Pine, painted red. Medieval-type benches such as this were used alongside the dining tables in peasant homes up to the 18th century. After the meal the back could be turned over, making the bench face the room. Knobs on the back fit into grooves in the legs to give steadiness. Similar benches often were used in churches.

Gothic style turn-over Bench from Uppland. Unpainted, made of pine and birch.

Medieval type of combination Chest and Bench from Småland, commonly used on the long side of the dining table. The bench, painted brown, has pink and white flowers with black leaves painted on blue panels. About 1800.

Above. Small oak Cupboard, dated 1646, with the owner's name, Sven Pederson, carved across the top, and his initials on the side. A Scriptural inscription is carved on the upper door, and on the lower door is IHS (*Iesus Hominum Salvator*).

Right. Cupboard showing a provincial translation of the Renaissance style. From Medelpad province. The trees are realistically painted green, with black trunks against a gray ground. Red, brown, yellow, and black paint accent the rest of the carving.

Above. Very fine and rare example of a Gothic style Cupboard, made about 1500. From the mining district in southern Dalarna province, which had a relatively refined manner of living for the 16th century. Painted dark brown, red and green, with iron mounts.

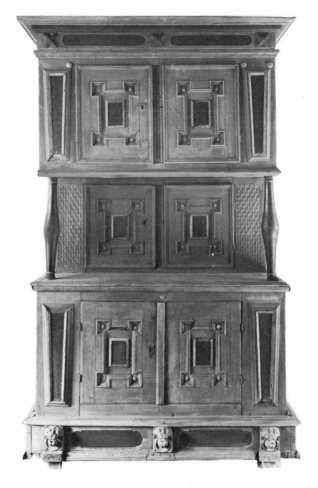

Above, left. Linen Cupboard of Baroque style fairly common in Sweden at the beginning of the 18th century, especially in the northern provinces. Painted grayish blue, with carved wooden applied ornaments painted red. From Medelpad.

Above. Large three-tiered Cupboard from Västmanland.

Left. Cupboard typical of central Sweden after about 1750, with rococo painting characterized by flowers and reticulated work. From Västmanland. 1775.

Detail of one of
the door panels.

Above. Provincial, Baroque style of Cupboard, decorated and signed by a well-known painter of wall paintings, Erik Eliasson. From Dalarna. 1780.

Right. An unusual type of Cupboard found only in the western parts of Sweden. The top shelves are left open. The back is decorated with painted floral and scroll design on a white ground. From Dalarna.

Excellent example of a type of painted Cupboard from Dalarna and a style which was widely spread over central Sweden. Dated 1786. A similar cupboard is shown placed in a room, on page 129.

Special local type of corner Cupboard, from Skåne, richly ornamented and painted blue, with red, yellow, white and green.

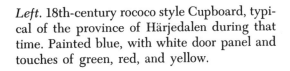

Left. 18th-century rococo style Cupboard, typical of the province of Härjedalen during that time. Painted blue, with white door panel and touches of green, red, and yellow.

Above. Hanging Cupboard from Hälsingland. The painting, however, is typical of Dalarna, where such pieces were made and sold to bordering provinces. Brown, with brush painting in reds, black, and white.

Left. A little Cupboard from Gästrikland, made and painted in Dalarna. Ground-color brown, with white, red, black, and green. Dated 1804.

Left. 17th-century Renaissance type of Table, from Halland. Used as a dining table. Linens were kept in the drawer and utensils in the lidded compartment below.

Above. Table from Härjedalen. Dated 1764. Sturdy tables of this construction were the most common type in the old peasant houses. It was used as the main table of the house and as the banquet table on feast days.

Left. 19th-century combination Table and Cupboard from Småland, a type made only in the southern provinces. Sometimes used as a dining table. Painted brown, with white flowers and black leaves painted on blue paneled doors. The top is black.

Above, right. Ancient form of stool, the *"Krakstol."* Made from a tree; the legs are roots or branches. From Jämtland. 1645.

Above, left. The *"Krakstol"* very often took fantastic forms. A few deft turns of the knife and an added tail gave this tree-trunk stool the shape of a dog. Dated 1843. From Jämtland.

Above. *"Kubbstol"* (block chair), made of the entire hollowed-out section of a tree trunk. One of the most ancient types of furniture. From Dalsland.

Left. Chair from Mora, Dalarna. Chairs of this type with varying backs were used in peasant homes in all parts of Sweden.

Above. Chair belonging to Swedish peasantry; the back was inspired by the Baroque chairs of the higher classes. This type of chair has been common for centuries in Swedish peasant homes. Made of pine and birch, painted brown, with Dalarnaian design in white, red, and black.

Above. Three-socket-legged Chair characteristic of the southern coastal province of Blekinge. Shows a Continental influence. Made of unpainted spruce and birch.

Left. "*Bordstol*" (table-chair) was, as the name implies, a combination of table and chair and was common in Swedish peasant houses. When used as a table, the back was turned down to make the fourth leg of the table. Pine, painted brown. From Södermanland.

Left. Early Medieval type of Chest from Häl-singland. Although it is 12th century, the decoration is a magnificent example of the old and very decorative art of the Viking Age (800-1050), a traditional design in many provinces. The very early chests had no lids.

Left. 13th-century Box for fleece or carded wool from Rättvik, Dalarna. The ornamentation can be traced to traditions deriving from prehistoric time and the Viking Age. A Detail of the dragon carving is shown.

Right. Chest from Härjeda-len. Earlier chests were not lidded. The decoration and construction is typical of the northeastern province during the 16th and 17th centuries.

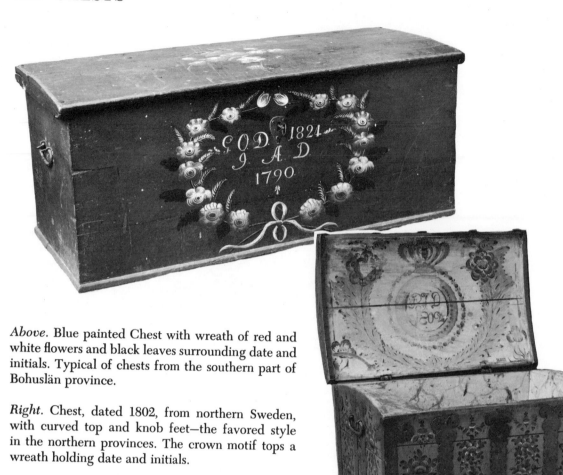

Above. Blue painted Chest with wreath of red and white flowers and black leaves surrounding date and initials. Typical of chests from the southern part of Bohuslän province.

Right. Chest, dated 1802, from northern Sweden, with curved top and knob feet—the favored style in the northern provinces. The crown motif tops a wreath holding date and initials.

Below. Fine example of rococo painting. Chest of oak, painted a light blue with painted scrolls and flowers. The frame is painted on. Dated 1815. From Skåne.

Right. Footed Chest from southern Skåne, typical of the southern coastal district where earthen floors were usual. The curved top, favored in southern and northern Sweden, was less common in the central provinces.

Left. Chest from the central province of Dalarna, where flat lids were more usual. The design of white, red, and green on a brown ground was done in 1861 by Mats Persson Stadig, who was also known for his wall paintings.

Left. Top of a wooden Trinket Box, with chip carving. From Småland. Dated 1734.

Above. This footed Box with a curved lid and handle is typical of the provinces of Småland and Västergötland. The front and top are painted white with relief design in red and black. The sides reverse the colors, with white and black against red.

Above. Painted Box dated 1827, from Hälsingland. The rather professional decorating was probably done by a wandering artist who went from farm to farm to decorate pieces the peasants had made during the long winter months.

Right. Quaint Trinket Box from the most northern Swedish province of Norrbotten. Dated 1828. Painted red, with ornaments in yellow, white, and blue.

Right. Delightful Box with flaring sides and twin-hearts design. From Hälsingland. One heart holds the date and the other a girl's initials. The box would contain the girl's trinkets and bits of ribbon.

Left. Box, painted red with flower design. The oval shape suggests that it probably was used to contain a head-dress. From Norrbotten. Dated 1856.

Right. Decorative Boxes with sloping lids, like this one, were the favored type in Södermanland province. This one is painted blue, with design in red, green, yellow, and white.

Above. 18th-century Clock, showing rococo style influence, as do most peasantry pieces from Jämtland and the bordering province of Härjedalen. Painted blue, with red, white, and black.

Right. Standing Clock, with flower painting, typical of the southern part of Bohuslän province. The case is painted blue-green, with red and white flowers and black leaves. The dial and ornaments on the iron dial-plate are lead. The owner's initials OHS and the date 1789 appear on the case. The clock-maker's initials MNYS are on the inside.

Above. This Clock, dated 1793, has an English type of case, following the example of upper-class importations, a trend which became apparent about 1700. The painting, however, is typical of Dalarna province. For characteristic placement, see this same clock in the interior of a peasant house on page 133.

Above. Clock made in 1808, in which the straight lines of the olden-type clock cases were retained, but the circular face, now white, was given a circular framing. The painting is brown, white, and black, and is done in the usual Dalarna manner. The dial is signed: Mats Matsson, Mora.

Right. The term *"Mora-klocka"* (a clock from Mora, Dalarna) especially applies to this type, with circular white dial and rounded case. Painted brown, with flowers in white, black, and green. Dated 1844.

Above. "Ångermanland Bride," a richly decorated Clock made by a famous joiner, Wåhlberg, from Sätra, Ångermanland. The bride's crown and all her wedding ornaments—neck ornament, hanging purse, bridal belt, etc. —are suggested in the wood carvings, which are painted red, white, yellow, and green. The case is painted grayish-green. The dial is signed A.A.S., the trademark of the famous Mora clock works. About 1820.

Left. Small unpainted Book Shelf from Härjedalen. The Biblical virgins are represented by two carved heads. The sad expression of the foolish one on the left contrasts with the happy expression of the wise virgin on the right. Probably made to hold prayer books.

Above. This Pipe-rack with drawer was hung in a corner. Made of birch, it comes from Västergötland.

Left. Small Shelf carved in a style which flourished in Ångermanland during the 18th century. Originally painted green.

Above. Butter Presses
from Härjedalen.

Above. Flour Ladle, from Jämtland.

Left. Pear-shaped Vessel, a milk-container
used on journeys. It hung by a leather shoul-
der-strap. Painted red, with blue, white, and
green, and the initials BOD AAS. From Mora,
Dalarna. Dated 1822.

Below. Box to hold flour, made in *"svep"* technique, with revolving lid. It is pear-shaped,
with a bird's head at the narrow end and decorative tail at the other. The decoration was
done with a burning-iron. From Jämtland.

Before Christmas all kinds of bread and cakes were baked for the "Christmas piles." There was one pile for each member of the family, and each cake in the pile was impressed with its special stamp. Cakes decorated with a stamp also played an important role on other festive days. At weddings decorated cakes were brought in by the bride after she had taken off her wedding dress and put on her "young mistress" dress. Each guest at funerals took such a cake home to keep as a remembrance.

Above. Wooden Spoon from Härjedalen, carved with a case knife. 1875.

Above. Front and back view of a Spoon from Uppland province with inscription: "Food in the Name of Jesus. Anno 1754. IPS."

Left. Ring-Spoon, dated 1843. A courtship spoon. Carved from one piece of wood. From Gästrikland.

In olden days, when a young Swedish peasant went courting, an elaborately carved wooden spoon was visible in the button-hole of his jacket, as a declaration of his intentions. When the girl saw the spoon she could be encouraging or discouraging as she felt inclined. The girls in return braided bits of bright-colored yarn to give to the boys, who flaunted the little dolls from their hats or wore them on their jackets. "You will have thread from me, if I get a spoon from you," was the saying.

Left. "*Snibbskål*," an early four-tipped Drinking Bowl painted red. From Östergötland. Inscription: "Drink and eat, but do not forget God, death, and the judgment."

Right. Footed, bird-shaped Drinking Cup which stood on the table beside the ale bowl. Head and tail form handles. From Härjedalen.

Above. "Ölgås" (beergoose) which floated in the great ale bowl. Guests dipped the "beergoose" into the ale and then drank from it. It is carved from birch, and painted black and gray with red crest. From Jämtland. Bird-shaped vessels occur mainly in northern Sweden.

Right. Beer Stoup from Dalarna. It is marked "Anders Andersson i [of] Lima 1865."

Above. Drinking Bowl with dragon-head handles. From Dalarna.

Above. Footed Tankard with knob decoration on the handle. From Småland.

Left. Tankard with spout, used to bring ale up from the barrels in the cellar. The design was burned in with an iron.

Left. Round "svepta" headdress Box with convex lid. Scratched pattern on light wood; a soot-rubbing darkened the incised lines. From Västerbotten.

Below. Small "svepta" Sewing Box with snap-on lid. Incised pattern on darkened wood. The natural color of the under light wood gives the design a special character. From Jämtland.

Above. Box carved from one piece of wood. With sliding lid. Used to hold a man's shaving equipment. Dated 1787, with initials MBS.

Right. Painted Box in "*svep*" technique. Probably a betrothal gift. From Skåne. 1769.

Left. Basket made with staves, to hang by the loom and hold bobbins. At berry-picking time it was taken along to hold berries.

Above. Woven chip Basket with painting. From Gästrikland. Dated 1866. In such baskets women carried to feasts gifts of bread prettily covered with an embroidered linen square.

Left. Basket made of roots elaborately woven to form a pattern. From Hälsingland.

Two details of a mural carved in wood by Robert Nilsson for a passenger liner of the Swedish-American Line, which burned just before the mural was installed. The mural has consequently been preserved.

A young Swedish sailor, returning from the sea, greets his Swedish maiden, and brings to her in his gear-bag the whole world of his voyaging. In the details shown here, which comprise less than half of the mural, Indonesian, Turkish, and African motifs are outstanding, in combination with a variety of marine symbols.

Murals executed in wood inlay for a building in Gothenburg are shown here as photographed in the studio of the artist, Ewald Dahlskog. A great variety of woods is employed to give the fullest possible range of contrasting natural colors, in a highly modern design of finest detail.

All three Doors were executed in modern wood inlay for the Town Hall of Halmstad, Sweden, and symbolize the cultural and industrial life of the coastal town.

In the design above at left, W. Lorenzon achieved, by the use of contrasting woods, an extraordinary effect of diaphanous delicacy in the draperies of the figures.

The door immediately above is the design of Stellan Mörner. Notable in the wealth of fine detail is the effect of a moiré fabric in the woman's gown.

The design at left, the work of Sven Jonson, makes use of the symbols of Justice.

Floral designs, one realistic, the other highly conventionalized, designed and executed in wood inlay on two chests by Carl Malmsten. Both show a remarkable union of artistry and technical skill.

Chests and a Chair by Joseph Frank, designer in several fields. The mahogany Chest above at left is fifty inches high. Flower prints are fixed to the surface and specially treated for durability. The treatment of the legs in both Chests is characteristic of Swedish modern. The drawers of the chest at right, by their intricate variety of size, make a pattern and are of wood inlay. The walnut Chair with leather seat is a notable combination of delicacy and strength.

All for Svenskt Tenn.

Right. Table decorations carved in Dalarna for the Hemslöjd. They make clever use of the natural knots of the wood.

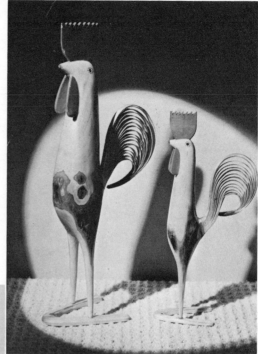

Left. "Bird" Fruit Bowls, made from birch in Ångermanland for the Hemslöjd.

Right. Heart-shaped wicker Bread-baskets, woven for the Hemslöjd in Gothenburg.

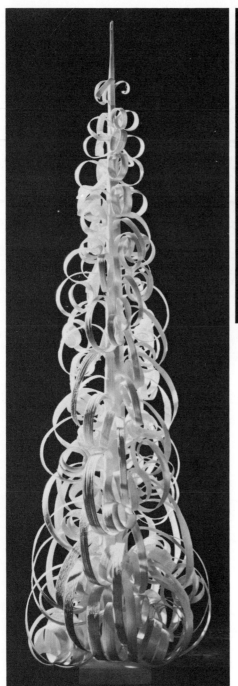

Above, Christmas Doves, whittled from thin wood, and intended for hanging as casual decorations.

Left. Table Decoration: a Christmás Tree whittled from one piece of wood.

Right. Snowflake Decorations, whittled from three strips of wood.

All for the Hemslöjd Association.

CHAPTER VII

WALL PAINTINGS

THE unique outstanding feature of Swedish folk culture is the kind of painting used in the wall decorations of the last two centuries. Although painted ceilings and walls, or traces of such decoration, are to be found all over Sweden, two districts produced most of the paintings. One of these, in southern Sweden, included Halland, parts of Småland, and parts of adjoining provinces. The other region was the province of Dalarna and neighboring provinces of central and northern Sweden. Paintings from these widely separated parts of the country had very little in common because of the different types of houses favored by the two districts. Since the paintings were done to suit the houses, two distinct types of wall decoration resulted.

In the southern region, the ancient dwelling house was still the leading type when, about 1730, painted hangings began partially to replace the ancient woven hangings. Attached to the exposed ridgepole and to the walls above the built-in benches in exactly the same way as the earlier woven hangings, they naturally acquired the same narrow and horizontally long form, since their size was determined by the spaces they were to fit. If the household had especially fine textile hangings, these were not discarded but simply hung side by side with the painted hangings. There could never be too many hangings for Christmas and for weddings; if the room resembled the inside of a tent, so much the better. After the festivities the paintings were taken down from the walls along with the woven hangings, and rolled and stored in cup-

boards or chests in the "chest-room," if the house could boast of this additional storage room. The hangings, woven or painted, were never left up for every-day decoration.

In Dalarna and northern Sweden, the typical house contained not a single room, but two large rooms, each having a fireplace. All daily living activities took place in one of the rooms. The other large room across from the entrance hall was used only on festive occasions; at other times it was left unheated and with the door closed. This large room had no beds, and no furniture other than that which would be used for a feast. Benches, usually movable ones, lined the walls. A turn-over bench by the long banquet table, a cupboard to hold special table service, and the traditional "seat of honor" were its complete furnishings. There was no rug on the floor, no curtains at the windows. Because the windows were large and there were many of them and the ceiling was high, this room was light and airy. It was the favored room. If the house had unfinished ceilings when it was built, the ceiling of this room was the first to be built as the prosperity of the family increased. Only after it was properly finished was attention given to the ceiling of the main room which was used every day. All artistic labor went into the decorating of the seldom-used "feast-day room." Its walls and ceilings were covered with paintings which were done directly on the walls and remained as permanent decorations.

The walls were first given a background of flat, grayish whitewash from which the colorful paintings stood out boldly. Occasionally the figures and floral decorations were painted on canvas or pasteboard which would then be permanently fixed to the walls. These paintings, like the ones in the South, conformed to spaces, but since the wall space was larger and the ceiling was finished, with no exposed rafters and beams to arrest the designs, they took on an entirely different character from those in southern Sweden. The spaces between windows and doors created panels on which large figures could be painted. Often painted drapes extended from the main motifs down to the baseboard, since movable benches were favored. The sloping but smooth surface of the ceiling allowed the artists greater freedom with floral motifs.

All peasant wall paintings, however, derive from the same sources: either from the painted interiors of medieval churches, or from the elaborately painted wall decorations in aristocratic homes and the slightly less elaborate wall decorations in middle-class houses of the Renaissance and Baroque periods. In some few cases certain rococo elements are to be found.

The painting was done in distemper on fine linen cloth or canvas. During the 19th century a heavy grayish paper or pasteboard was used. In order to make the paintings long enough, it often was necessary to piece the linen or to paste several pieces of paper together before the work could begin.

Although the artists were professional painters, they were of the same social level as the peasants and led the same sort of life as other peasants. A few of them had been part-time soldiers, with opportunity to travel a bit, to see paintings in churches and draw inspiration from these. Some of the painters were farmers, but their tracts of land would be so small or so poor as to make painting a more profitable occupation, if they had a talent for such work. Others were descendants of painters, and sometimes there were whole families of painters, both men and women. In Sunnerbo, in the south of Småland, four generations of one family were painters. The first of these was born in 1741, and the last painting by a member of this family was done in 1870; the family group numbered sixteen and produced many paintings.

During the long, cold winters the painters worked at home on the orders they had taken the summer before. In the summer they traveled the countryside, delivering work and acquiring fresh commissions for the next winter. Often they carried samples of the canvas or paper they intended to use, and many of the paintings show on their reverse sides the details of the business transaction. The customer's name, the subjects he wanted executed, the size of the painting, when it was to be delivered, and the price, these were notes which the painter jotted down on the backs of the paintings.

Because of the space-filling requirements, it was necessary that the paintings be made to order. When an artist paid a visit to his peasant-farmer client, the two would review the paintings the household already had and would note their subject matter, in order that the new painting should not repeat narratives already illustrated, or at least should not repeat them too many times. After the question of subject matter had been settled, size was the next consideration. Any space on the ceiling or walls which old paintings did not cover would determine this. It was a part of the painter's job to take measurements of the open spaces and make his motifs conform to them—triangular, to fit up into the top of the gable-end wall; deep and wide, for the walls behind benches; or very long and narrow, to go between shelves or to fit into rafter spaces.

Painters in the northernmost parts of Sweden worked in much the same manner as those in the southern districts, but in central Dalarna and in neighboring provinces, where painting was done directly on the walls, the artist would be a guest of the household while he did his work.

All painters derived the great majority of their motifs from Biblical history. Very often the whole scene, the arrangement of the figures, their attitudes, the various appurtenances required to make clear what was going on, in fact, everything in the picture, would be inspired by illustrations in Bibles and hymn-books, or by religious prints. Some of the compositions go back to medieval church paintings, but, Sweden being a protestant country and the peasants very orthodox, no saint is to be seen except Saint George, and the dragon. Of course the drawing is summary and everything greatly simplified. The holy men and women are dressed in costumes worn by the burghers and peasants of the Sweden of the time, a detail which often creates a bizarre effect: one sees the children of Israel dressed like the men and women of Dalarna, and the Saviour wears a Swedish clergyman's gown. Such allegories as "The Ages of Man," legendary heroes and historical characters, such as Napoleon and the Royal Family of Sweden, all were treated in the same delightfully incongruous manner. Hunting scenes and pictures of more or less exotic animals are common, but rural or domestic scenes out of the life of the peasantry are rare.

Though the number of motifs is sharply limited and the manifestation on the whole is strictly bound by tradition, it is easy to distinguish both prominent artistic personalities and what might be called different schools of painting.

Of the painters in the northern provinces, Gustaf Reuter (1699-1783) was one of the earliest. He and his successors worked in Hälsingland, and a number of houses decorated by him still stand. His painting was done directly on the white walls and resembles old church paintings, not only because of his style of drawing but because of the colors he used: grey, yellow, red, and black on white. Some of the Hälsingland wall painters had apparently studied the wall decorations painted in oil in the homes of the higher classes, for the drawing is more naturalistic and the colors more shaded and refined. Many of these painted interiors in southern Hälsingland have been preserved also.

It is the paintings from central Dalarna, however, which are the most renowned in Sweden, and some excellent poetry has been written about them by Sweden's popular poet, E. A. Karlfeldt. The peculiar Dalarnaian style was developed about 1780. Huge floral motifs characterize these paintings. In all peasant painting, flowers and ornaments unrelated to the narrative which is being depicted fill up the empty spaces between the figures. In Dalarna the size of the flowers was gradually increased until in the composition they became fully as important as the figures. These huge, close bunches of fantastic flowers are called "*kurbits*"—a name supposedly derived from the Biblical scene in which Jonah sat in the desert outside Niniveh and the Lord caused a "*kurbits*," a gourd vine (*cucurbita*), to grow up behind him, thus saving his life by protecting his head from the sun.

The Dalarnaian paintings are generally divided into the Rättvik and the Leksand schools. At least forty painters are known from each school, but each of them had his individual style. Farms with one or more rooms decorated by a Leksand or Rättvik painter are still to be seen in Dalarna and all neighboring provinces.

The Dalarnaians, especially in Rättvik, also painted and sold furniture, mostly cupboards. The conventionalized flowers on the cupboard panels are executed in much the same style as those in the wall paintings.

In southern Sweden, in the eastern part of Småland, the painted wall hangings were very long, sometimes extending the entire width of the wall. The colors were dark, and various scenes from Bible stories were separated by decorative columns. Very often a hunting scene or a row of animals or conventionalized flowers formed a lower border.

In Halland and in the western part of Småland the paintings had a style that by 1730 was fully developed, becoming traditional in all later hangings. The long, narrow space was filled by many scenes out of the same story. The narratives chosen were full of action, for example, the story of Joseph and his brethren. By far the most popular subjects were the parable of the wise and foolish virgins, the wedding at Cana, and the adoration of the Christ child by the three wise men.

Each painter had his own style of painting, and his own favorite motifs and complementary flowers and borders. Some were good colorists, others were not. Some painters had a special gift for depicting humorous scenes, such as the farmer on his way to market to sell his oxen; before he gets there he meets another farmer who gets the better of him in an exchange of animals. Another popular subject was that of a man going to a fair on a horse; he usually meets another man and exchanges blows, although why is never quite clear. But the religious paintings were what the peasants preferred in their homes, especially the Christmas gospel. Johannes Nilsson (1757-1827), who was a highly religious man as well as a talented artist, executed many of the religious paintings.

Many thousands of paintings, from the end of the 18th century to the last quarter of the 19th century, are to be found in official and private collections in Sweden today.

Below is the inner gable wall of the interior of a peasant house from the south of Sweden which has been reassembled in the open-air museum at Jönköping. Above the *rya*-covered bench hangs a Wall Painting which presents the popular Scriptural theme of the ten virgins, who took their lamps and went forth to meet the bridegroom. Above the virgins is another favored theme in wall paintings—that of the Three Wise Men, all ahorse, and bound for Bethlehem in Swedish peasant garb. The Christmas gospel was a rich source of subjects for paintings designed to be hung especially at Christmas. Over the curtained bed at left, smaller paintings can be seen tacked to the sloping rafters.

Shown here also are some of the woven shelf-hangings described in the chapter on Textiles. The narrower ones end in two-color fringe.

Above is the interior of a Blekinge cottage, a typical main room from that southern province. It has now been reassembled at the open-air museum of Skansen, Stockholm. On the inner gable wall are two Wall Hangings, by different painters, which cover the open space up to the very peak; they are separated by a shelf which holds tankards. Other furnishings shown in the photograph are characteristic. The built-in dining benches with woven covers are straw-filled to provide insulation. The three-legged chairs have already been mentioned as especially typical of Blekinge. From a beam a child's hanging chair is suspended by a pole. On the table is a wooden meatstand and iron candlesticks. Behind the table is a corner cupboard which is attached to the wall and rests on the bench. It is edged with a woven hanging, and the festive hangings over the window are also woven.

Right. A close-up of the corner of the room shows the detail of the Wall Painting and the construction of the trestle table. In the painting, the Virgin, holding the Infant Jesus, receives gifts from the Wise Men. Above are the five wise virgins.

Above. Wall Painting from Småland, dated 1763. Painted by Nils Svensson.

The parable of the ten virgins was as popular a subject in wall paintings as in textiles. The five foolish virgins (Matthew, XXV), lined up on the left, hold lamps without oil. Receding smoke clouds in the distance show that the lamps have gone out. The virgins' small crowns are blackened and sit askew on their heads. The curl has gone from their hair. which hangs in straight locks. Flowers growing between the foolish virgins have wilted.

This depressing scene is cheerfully balanced by the five wise virgins, who stand with lamps ablaze. Their hair is in curl, and large golden crowns sit proudly on their heads. Vigorously growing flowers bloom between them.

In the small panel at far left, the sleeping Elijah is visited by the angel.

Any leftover space on the painting was often filled with a hunting scene composed of animals of various kinds and sizes, chased by hunting dogs and running head-on into the hunter's fire, as shown here and on the painting below.

Below. Another Wall Painting by Nils Svensson. Dated 1795.
In the small panel at left we have Jonah with the "gourd" overhead. The structure at right of him represents Nineveh in the distance. (Jonah, IV.)
In the next panel is a version of the angel appearing to Abraham, who is about to sacrifice his son Isaac. (Genesis, XXII.)

The long panel shows the marriage feast in Cana of Galilee and follows the pattern of any typical Swedish wedding portrayal, except for the added table, the stone waterpots, and the merry-making guests. Jesus stands at the extreme right. Seated at the table is Mary, His Mother, wearing a crown and much finery. To Her right, disciples drink a toast. The six stone pots below hold the water that was turned into wine. (John, II.)

At bottom is the space-filling hunting scene.

This Wall Painting from Skåne, dated 1782, is attributed to the Nils Svensson of the two preceding paintings.

In the upper left-hand panel is Abraham, about to sacrifice his son Isaac, who kneels on a flower altar; the angel stays the knife and points to the ram "caught in a thicket by his horns." (Genesis, XXII.) The upper right-hand panel, possibly conceived as the Wedding in Cana, did not develop beyond the typical Swedish peasant wedding scene. The bride and groom dance to music, while her parents serve ale to guests who do not enter the picture. In the lower tier of panels we have, at the far left, Jonah sitting under the protective vine at Nineveh; next, an angel points out the well of water to Hagar with her son Ishmael in the wilderness of Beersheba; the Infant Jesus, wrapped in swaddling clothes, lies in the manger between Joseph and Mary; and finally, an angel brings cake and water to Elijah, asleep under the juniper tree (I Kings, XIX).

In the Wall Paintings of southern Sweden, perpendicular decorative columns always separate the story panels.

Left. Fragment of a gable-end Wall Painting. From Småland. Painted by Nils Svensson and his son, Johannes Nilsson.

Upper panel: Elijah is fed by ravens (I Kings) and is borne to heaven in a chariot of fire while his mantle falls to Elisha (II Kings).

Lower panel: "Belshazzar the king made a great feast" (Daniel, V).

The moon looks down disapprovingly at Adam and Eve in the garden of Eden as they eat the fruit of the tree. They hold "aprons" made of sewed fig leaves. (Genesis, III.)

A cook, with pipe, prepares the repast for the wedding feast in Cana of Galilee. (John, II.) The disciples are present but Jesus and Mary are not, probably due to lack of space. On the neatly set table is a traditional Swedish egg-cake.

Jesus rides into Jerusalem while a "great multitude spread their garments in the way; others cut down branches from the trees, and strawed them in the way" (Matthew, XXI). A Detail is shown below.

Painted by Johannes Nilsson, 1757-1827.

David, with a sling and stone, is about to slay Goliath. (I Samuel, XVII.)

Absalom, whose hair is caught in the "thick boughs of a great oak," is slain by Joab. At the right is King David receiving the message in "the chamber over the gate." (II Samuel, XVIII.)

Saint George and the dragon.

From Halland. Painted by Nils Svensson, 1727-1802.

In the lower of the two paintings above, the Three Wise Men, in Swedish attire, approach Bethlehem on horseback, each separated from his fellow by a decorative column. The dividing column becomes a church, and next we see them presenting their gifts of gold, frankincense, and myrrh to "the young child with Mary his mother." (Matthew, II.) Joseph stands behind Mary's chair.

The long panel across the bottom shows another representation of the parable of the ten virgins. From Halland. Dated 1775. Painted by Nils Lundberg.

Below, the priests are encompassing the city of Jericho. Four of them blow ram's-horn trumpets, while two carry the ark. The walls of Jericho are shown in process of falling down. (Joshua, VI).

The adjacent panel shows the Last Supper. The table is set in typical Swedish peasant style. From Halland. Dated 1775. Painted by Johannes Nilsson.

Below. A wedding has just taken place in the church. The newly married couple depart for the reception feast at the bride's home, where she will change her bridal crown and elaborately embroidered wedding dress for her "young mistress" dress and will serve traditional fancy little cakes to all the guests. Sitting rather precariously in the first carriage, she holds her wedding bouquet and wears a traditional silver neck ornament with three chains. Behind her sits the groom, also with a bouquet. Two outrider attendants follow. Next come the six bridesmaids in a carriage drawn by two dappled horses. Well-wishers stand by the church. They wave cheerfully, but their expressions show due ceremonial solemnity.

Section of a Wall Painting from Halland, painted by Per Svensson. Dated 1838.

Above. The same painter shows another wedding party at a more advanced stage of the festivities. They are returning to the bride's home for the wedding feast. Here the groom faces the bride in their carriage. The wedding couple and the bridesmaids are preceded by musicians and important guests on an assortment of horses in stripes, polka dots, and bright, solid color. Two guests stand in front of the house ready to drink a toast. The woman carries a basket with the traditional gift of food, covered with an embroidered linen square. In the center of the painting is the "wedding gate," completely covered with flowers, a custom still observed in rural Sweden today. Worthy of special note in both paintings is the space-filling detail.

From Halland. Painted by Per Svensson.

Above is a Wall Painting from Halland by Sven Persson, 1776-1841. In the upper half, the panel at the far left depicts Adam and Eve. The six waterpots of stone, which held the water that was turned to wine, lead us into a panel showing the wedding feast in Cana of Galilee.

In the lower half, St. George, at far left, battles the dragon; next is the representation of an old Swedish folk-song in which the Dane and Burman duel; then, in order, Samson rends the lion with his bare hands, David prepares to slay Goliath, and Jonah sits beneath the gourd vine outside Nineveh.

At left is a Detail of David and Goliath, and below a Detail of the wedding guests in Cana.

Right. Again the wedding feast in Cana of Galilee. The table bears a whole fish and a roasted whole pig. Beneath the table are the inevitable six water-pots.

In the lower panel Elijah, departing for heaven in a whirlwind and chariot and horses of fire, drops his mantle to Elisha.

Painted by Anders Eriksson, 1774-1840.

Left. The painter who conceived this representation of David and Goliath intended to leave the beholder in no doubt as to their relative sizes. The flowers are an outstanding example of the decorative "kurbits" motif developed from the story of Jonah outside Nineveh.

Across the top of the two facing pages and concluded immediately above is a long Wall Painting from Halland, shown here in its entirety. It was painted by Anders Pålsson (1781-1849). At the left is Elisha sending the young man to Ramothgilead with the box of oil to anoint Jehu. In the next panel, the king in his carriage, followed by guards, points to the three eunuchs who peer from the windows before throwing Jezebel, her of the painted face, down to the dogs below.

The heads of Ahab's seventy slain sons lie in a heap at the gate; other heads are in a basket to be sent to Jezreel. In the final panel the heads are viewed the next morning. (II Kings, X.)

A Detail of the King's guards is shown on the right-hand page.

A story out of the life of the peasantry, unusual as a theme for a Wall Painting. A farmer goes to market to sell his two oxen. He meets a man and sells one ox. Continuing his way, he meets a second man and exchanges his ox for a horse. Riding on, he meets a man on a horse. They dismount and exchange blows, for no apparent reason. Our hero takes his defeated opponent, who is staggering, and panting for breath, to a tavern and buys him a drink. (The wine shop has the usual wrought-iron wreath of grapes and leaves hanging over the door.) A decorative column writes finis to this sequence.

In town, the farmer leads his girl by the hand to a glove shop and buys her a pair of gloves. He goes alone to buy a new hat for himself.

Painted by Erik Andersson, 1774-1840. From Småland.

A Painting from Halland, executed by Anders Pålsson in a shape unusual among wall paintings in the south of Sweden, deals with the adventures of Joseph. *Top.* Potiphar's wife "caught him by his garment, saying, Lie with me: and he left his garment in her hand, and fled . . ." (Genesis, XXXIX, 12). *Center.* "And there passed by Midianites merchantmen; and they drew and lifted up Joseph out of the pit, and sold Joseph to the Ishmaelites . . ." (Genesis, XXXVII, 28). *Bottom.* "And they sent the coat of many colours, and they brought it to their father; and said, This have we found: know now whether it be thy son's coat or no . . ." (Genesis, XXXVII, 32).

A casual, humorous Wall Painting, done by Per Svensson probably as a random space-filler. The inscription over the man in uniform says, "Have you ever seen the like [of me]?"

Two decorative Paintings which tell no special story, though they may have been inspired by traditional representations of the Three Wise Men. The corner of the lower one has been worn away. Both are interesting for space-filling details and the rich coloring that characterizes them. The paintings probably were the work of a member of the third generation of the Sunnerbo school. More of the work of this school is shown on the following pages.

Four Wall Paintings from the Sunnerbo school, which comprised sixteen painters of four generations of one family (1741-1870). The drawing of the hair, and the wide decorative columns (never duplicated in respect to color) between the panels, are two distinguishing features of the school. Of the four examples shown here, the second from the top, done by Nils Persson (1772-1836), who was of the second generation, may be considered as typical. He used Biblical stories not often encountered in the work of painters outside the Sunnerbo influence. The Scriptural references above the panels indicate their inspiration. From left to right:

"Let this cup pass from me!" The Disciples sleep, still wearing their Swedish hats. (Matthew, XXVI, 39.)

The woman of Canaan cries that her daughter is grievously vexed with a devil. (Matthew, XV, 22.)

The hypocrite is told not to behold the mote in his brother's eye but to perceive the beam in his own. (Matthew, VII, 5).

"Come unto me, all ye that labour and are heavy laden, and I will give you rest." (Matthew, XI, 28.)

The Ten Commandments.

Three of these subjects are treated also in the topmost painting. In the lowest painting, which illustrates the Birth of Christ, decorative church fronts separate the scenes.

Above. Detail of one panel of the topmost painting.

Left. The angel appears to Hagar and her son in the wilderness of Beersheba to reveal the well of water. (Genesis,XXI.) By Nils Persson. From Småland. 1794.

Two panels from a fragment by Nils Persson. From Småland. 1796.

The horses supposedly are those of Joseph's brothers.

Zacchaeus climbs a sycamore tree the better to see Jesus as he passes. (Luke,XIX.)

Since no part of the wall or ceiling was allowed to remain exposed on festive occasions, many of the less important spaces were covered with repeating floral paintings, such as this one.

Wall Painting from Småland, by Gudmund Nilsson, of the third generation of the Sunnerbo school. Dated 1839.

An angel appears to Mary and says, "blessed art thou among women." (Luke, I, 28.)

The Christ Child in the manger with the star of Bethlehem overhead. (Luke, II, 7.)

Joseph and Mary take Jesus to Jerusalem. (Luke, II, 22.)

Angels guard the Christ Child while Joseph and Mary sleep. An angel appears to Joseph in a dream and tells him to flee into Egypt with Mary and the Child. (Matthew, II, 13.)

Joseph, Mary and the Child resting on their journey into Egypt. (Matthew, II, 14.)

Jesus at the age of twelve is taken to Jerusalem. (Luke, II, 42.)

At right and below are Details of several of the panels.

Above. The large scale of this Wall Painting of the ten virgins brings into prominence many of the features by which the "wise" were differentiated from the "foolish." One example is their silver neck lockets with many chains.

On the facing page, below, is the angel's visit to Mary. (Luke, I, 28.) Mary salutes Elisabeth. (Luke, I, 40.) Christ is born. "For, behold, I bring you good tidings of great joy." (Luke, II, 10.)

Below. Horses which carried Joseph's brothers when they came to Egypt to see him. Each horse nibbles hay in a separate stall, and in the Wall Painting each is a different, bright color.

Above. Again the wedding feast in Cana of Galilee. Musicians and dancers are in the foreground. The men at the well are drawing the water that was turned to wine. Jesus' halo has taken on the appearance of a fur hood. Mary sits serenely at the table's center wearing a crown.

The horse-drawn carriage embodies the inscription: "As you journey through life think of your last journey."

King Solomon, attended by guardsmen, is visited by the Queen of Sheba with servants who carry gifts. (I Kings, X.) The inscription translates: "The Queen of the rich Arabia visits King Solomon to hear his wisdom and see his gloriousness."

The space-filling hunting scene in more realistic than most. The animals are running away from the hunter's fire. Two dogs work for the hunter.

Below. Joseph's brothers come to see him in Egypt. (Genesis, XLII.) Probably by some painter of the Sunnerbo school.

"And these three men, Shadrach, Meshach, and Abed-nego, fell down bound into the midst of the burning fiery furnace." (Daniel, III, 23.) At the far right is Daniel in the lion's den.

In this Wall Painting from Halland, dated 1815, the popular subject of the wedding feast in Cana is supplemented (below) by scenes from the story of Jacob. In the two panels at left are Zilpah and her sons Gad and Asher, and Bilhah and her sons, Dan and Naphtali. (Genesis, XXX.)

In the right-hand panel, Jacob greets his brother Esau. Each man with a spear represents one hundred of the four hundred men who came with Esau. (Genesis, XXXIII.)

Across the bottom is an inscription from Proverbs, IX, 10: "The fear of the Lord is the beginning of wisdom: and the knowledge of the holy is understanding."

Below. Detail of a Wall Painting of the Three Wise Men. From Småland.

The Wall Paintings in Dalarna and neighboring northern provinces differed greatly from those in southern Sweden, due to the differences in the types of houses favored in the two sections and the function of the room which the paintings decorated.

In central and northern Sweden the houses contained two large rooms separated by an entrance hall. Both rooms had fireplaces. All daily living took place in one of the rooms. The other room across the hall never served as a "spare-room" or a room to hold numerous chests and the overflow of clothes hung on racks from the ceiling, as in southern Sweden. It was used only for festive occasions, and the furnishings were those pieces which would be needed for a great feast, such as movable benches along the walls, a large cupboard to hold special table service, the long banquet table, and the traditional "seat of honor." Wall paintings covered ceilings and walls, but unlike the ones in southern Sweden, they were done directly on the walls and remained as a permanent decoration. The painting was done in distemper on the whitewashed surfaces of wall and ceiling boards, or on canvas or pasteboard permanently fixed to the walls. The much higher ceiling, the comparatively large windows

and the sealed surfaces offered better lighting conditions and more unbroken spaces for artistic labor than did the low walls, small windows, and surfaces broken by rafters in the southern peasant homes. Since the wall paintings were made to conform to space, the paintings from the two sections had entirely different characteristics.

The photograph above shows the interior of a farm house from Hälsingland, now in the open-air museum in Skansen. The walls and ceilings were decorated by Gustaf Reuter (1699-1783). The man depicted near the door is to be found under various names in many old painted interiors. He is always intended to guard the entrance, and very often he has a heavy stick in his hand, sometimes a sword. Beside this one is written: "My name is Knut, if anyone doesn't behave himself, I will throw him out." Often a woman is painted on the opposite side of the door with a filled glass in her hand in token of welcome.

Floral motifs are prominent here. In the paintings shown in the following pages, the floral motifs become more important, overshadowing the narrative subject.

Wall Painting from Dalarna by Jufwas Anders Ersson (1757-1834), of the Leksand school. Mostly red and blue on white. Here are the ages of man, from the cradle to ninety.

A woman of Canaan seeks Christ's mercy on her daughter vexed by a devil. By Winter Carl Hansson (1777-1805), of the Leksand school. From a house in Dalarna.

Larshans Per Olsson (1786-1863), of the Leksand school, depicts a romantic encounter under an inscription which begins: "Good day, my friend and rose." From Härjedalen.

"Here you are going to see the workshop of one who makes shoes" is the inscription of this Wall Painting by Hjelt Per Persson (1821-1886), a late exponent of the Leksand school. From Dalarna.

Back Olof Andersson (1767-1820) executed in 1805, perhaps for a tavern-keeper, what was probably a wholly fanciful conception of a "wineyard"—its proprietor, laborers, and pay-office. Leksand school. From Dalarna.

Old maids saying, "Do you recognize us?" emerge rejuvenated from a beauty-mill in this Wall Painting by Hjelt Per Persson (1821-1886), of the Leksand school. From Dalarna.

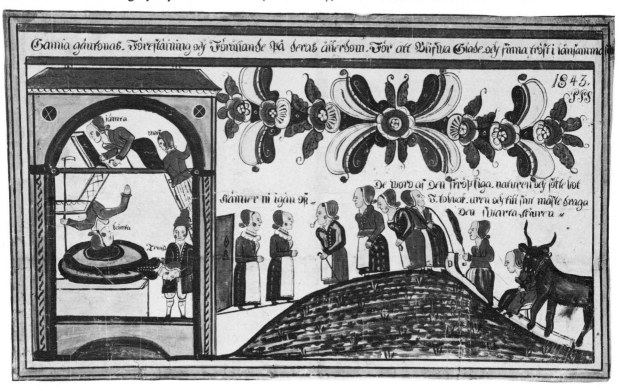

"Would You Like to Buy My Horse?" Snarf Anders Andersson (1795-1850), of the Leksand school, embellished the idea with a dominant floral motif. From Dalarna.

The ten virgins, five wise and five unwise, in the parable preached by Jesus. Kers Erik Jönsson (1805-1851, Leksand school) was the painter. The horizontal decorative borders at top and bottom were as characteristic of the Wall Paintings of the north as the decorative columns separating panels were typical of those of the south. Often the border served as a signature.

Above. In free translation: "Good day, brother—how would you like to change that big horse of yours? . . . Well, if you have the money, loosen up! One hundred in cash and it's yours. . . . That does it!" Back Erik Andersson (Leksand school) painted it in 1819 in his home village of Ullvi. From Hälsingland.

Right. The same roving painter executed the subject which accompanies the inscription: "We are going to enjoy ourselves for a while." From Dalarna.

Left. Karl Johan, the first Swedish king of the French line of Bernadotte, was the subject of a Wall Painting by Back Erik Andersson in 1831. From Dalarna.

Right. In 1819 Andersson depicted three women mourners at the tomb of Christ crucified. Also from Dalarna.

Some artisan of Dalarna engaged Back Erik Andersson to decorate his home and glorify his occupation in a Wall Painting which sets forth the inscription: "I am a bricklayer. Hurry up with bricks and mortar."

Left. A Biblical subject often met in southern Wall Paintings here is encountered in Dalarna in the work of Mats Anders Olsson (1824-1878), of the Rättvik school. Elijah, caught up to heaven in a chariot of fire, casts his mantle to Elisha. Executed in 1861.

Right. From Västmanland comes this Wall Painting by Lisserkers Olof Olofsson (1803-1874), also of the Rättvik school. It shows the "Queen of wealthy Arabia" (Sheba) coming to test King Solomon with riddles. Olofsson painted it at the age of nineteen.

Impressively embellished in floral and crown motifs by Lars Larsson of the Rättvik school, the Three Wise Men ride out of the East to attend the Christ Child in his manger. The Wall Painting is from Hälsingland, and Larsson signed it in 1824.

Godag min ädla ros och sköna Fröken.

Left. Some unidentified painter of the Rättvik school indulged in a moment of pure romanticism. "Good day, my noble rose and beautiful lady." From Dalarna.

Right. Flower painting from Dalarna by an artist of the Rättvik school. Symmetrical floral compositions of this type are to be found on Dalarnaian furniture.

An unknown painter of the Rättvik school who signed his works A.H.S. executed this floral panel, which is one of a complete set for a room. From Hälsingland.

These floral panels were signed in 1805 by A.H.S., the same unidentified painter of the early Rättvik school. At right is a detail of the narrow central panel.

As in the panel by this artist on the preceding page, a definite French influence is evident.

An unknown painter of the early Rättvik school executed this painting for the gable wall of a house in Dalarna. The central panel seems to depict the conversion of Saul on the road to Damascus. At left is a Detail of the left-hand panel.

A painter who signed his work O.W.S. in the year 1838 but who is otherwise unknown addressed himself to a time-honored subject. "The princess is delivered [by] the noble St. George who fought the dragon." From Dalarna.

The same unknown painter, signing his work in the same year, pictures the moment which precedes the Miracle of the Sea of Galilee. "Jesus is sleeping," says the inscription, "a great storm comes up, and the waves roll over the ship." From Dalarna.

Lars Rytarre (1800-1865), who was born in Rättvik and executed most of his professional work in the south of Dalarna, signed in 1830 this Wall Painting of Jesus riding into Jerusalem. From Gästrikland. It is interesting to compare this with a southern painter's treatment of the same subject on page 176.

INDEX

INDEX

Dover Books on Art

PRINCIPLES OF ART HISTORY, H. Wölfflin. This remarkably instructive work demonstrates the tremendous change in artistic conception from the 14th to the 18th centuries, by analyzing 164 works by Botticelli, Dürer, Hobbema, Holbein, Hals, Titian, Rembrandt, Vermeer, etc., and pointing out exactly what is meant by "baroque," "classic," "primitive," "picturesque," and other basic terms of art history and criticism. "A remarkable lesson in the art of seeing," SAT. REV. OF LITERATURE. Translated from the 7th German edition. 150 illus. 254pp. 6⅛ x 9¼. 20276-3 Paperbound $3.50

FOUNDATIONS OF MODERN ART, A. Ozenfant. Stimulating discussion of human creativity from paleolithic cave painting to modern painting, architecture, decorative arts. Fully illustrated with works of Gris, Lipchitz, Léger, Picasso, primitive, modern artifacts, architecture, industrial art, much more. 226 illustrations. 368pp. 6⅛ x 9¼. 20215-1 Paperbound $5.00

METALWORK AND ENAMELLING, H. Maryon. Probably the best book ever written on the subject. Tells everything necessary for the home manufacture of jewelry, rings, ear pendants, bowls, etc. Covers materials, tools, soldering, filigree, setting stones, raising patterns, repoussé work, damascening, niello, cloisonné, polishing, assaying, casting, and dozens of other techniques. The best substitute for apprenticeship to a master metalworker. 363 photos and figures. 374pp. 5½ x 8½. 22702-2 Paperbound $4.00

SHAKER FURNITURE, E. D. and *F. Andrews.* The most illuminating study of Shaker furniture ever written. Covers chronology, craftsmanship, houses, shops, etc. Includes over 200 photographs of chairs, tables, clocks, beds, benches, etc. "Mr. & Mrs. Andrews know all there is to know about Shaker furniture," Mark Van Doren, NATION. 48 full-page plates. 192pp. 7⅞ x 10¾. 20679-3 Paperbound $4.00

LETTERING AND ALPHABETS, J. A. Cavanagh. An unabridged reissue of "Lettering," containing the full discussion, analysis, illustration of 89 basic hand lettering styles based on Caslon, Bodoni, Gothic, many other types. Hundreds of technical hints on construction, strokes, pens, brushes, etc. 89 alphabets, 72 lettered specimens, which may be reproduced permission-free. 121pp. 9¾ x 8. 20053-1 Paperbound $2.75

THE HUMAN FIGURE IN MOTION, Eadweard Muybridge. The largest collection in print of Muybridge's famous high-speed action photos. 4789 photographs in more than 500 action-strip-sequences (at shutter speeds up to 1/6000th of a second) illustrate men, women, children—mostly undraped—performing such actions as walking, running, getting up, lying down, carrying objects, throwing, etc. "An unparalleled dictionary of action for all artists," AMERICAN ARTIST. 390 full-page plates, with 4789 photographs. Heavy glossy stock, reinforced binding with headbands. 7⅞ x 10¾. 20204-6 Clothbound $13.50

THE FOUR BOOKS OF ARCHITECTURE, Andrea Palladio.
A compendium of the art of Andrea Palladio, one of the most
celebrated architects of the Renaissance, including 250 mag-
nificently-engraved plates showing edifices either of Palladio's
design or reconstructed (in these drawings) by him from classical ruins and contemporary accounts. 257 plates. xxiv + 119pp.
9½ x 12¾.   21308-0 Paperbound $8.95

150 MASTERPIECES OF DRAWING, A. Toney. Selected by a
gifted artist and teacher, these are some of the finest drawings
produced by Western artists from the early 15th to the end of
the 18th centuries. Excellent reproductions of drawings by Rembrandt, Bruegel, Raphael, Watteau, and other familiar masters,
as well as works by lesser known but brilliant artists. 150 plates.
xviii + 150pp. 5⅜ x 11¼.   21032-4 Paperbound $4.00

MORE DRAWINGS BY HEINRICH KLEY. Another collection
of the graphic, vivid sketches of Heinrich Kley, one of the most
diabolically talented cartoonists of our century. The sketches
take in every aspect of human life: nothing is too sacred for him
to ridicule, no one too eminent for him to satirize. 158 drawings
you will not easily forget. iv + 104pp. 7⅜ x 10¾.
                              20041-8 Paperbound $3.75

*THE TRIUMPH OF MAXIMILIAN I, 137 Woodcuts by Hans
Burgkmair and Others.* This is one of the world's great art
monuments, a series of magnificent woodcuts executed by the
most important artists in the German realms as part of an
elaborate plan by Maximilian I, ruler of the Holy Roman Empire,
to commemorate his own name, dynasty, and achievements. 137
plates. New translation of descriptive text, notes, and bibliography prepared by Stanley Appelbaum. Special section of 10pp.
containing a reduced version of the entire Triumph. x + 169pp.
11⅛ x 9¼.   21207-6 Paperbound $5.95

PAINTING IN ISLAM, Sir Thomas W. Arnold. This scholarly
study puts Islamic painting in its social and religious context
and examines its relation to Islamic civilization in general. 65
full-page plates illustrate the text and give outstanding examples
of Islamic art. 4 appendices. Index of mss. referred to. General
Index. xxiv + 159pp. 6⅝ x 9¼.   21310-2 Paperbound $4.00

*THE MATERIALS AND TECHNIQUES OF MEDIEVAL
PAINTING, D. V. Thompson.* An invaluable study of carriers
and grounds, binding media, pigments, metals used in painting,
al fresco and al secco techniques, burnishing, etc. used by the
medieval masters. Preface by Bernard Berenson. 239pp. 5⅜ x 8.
                              20327-1 Paperbound $3.50

*THE HISTORY AND TECHNIQUE OF LETTERING, A.
Nesbitt.* A thorough history of lettering from the ancient Egyp-
tians to the present, and a 65-page course in lettering for artists.
Every major development in lettering history is illustrated by a
complete aphabet. Fully analyzes such masters as Caslon, Koch,
Garamont, Jenson, and many more. 89 alphabets, 165 other specimens. 317pp. 7½ x 10½.   20427-8 Paperbound $5.00

200 DECORATIVE TITLE-PAGES, edited by A. Nesbitt. Fascinating and informative from a historical point of view, this beautiful collection of decorated titles will be a great inspiration to students of design, commercial artists, advertising designers, etc. A complete survey of the genre from the first known decorated title to work in the first decades of this century. Bibliography and sources of the plates. 222pp. 8⅜ x 11¼.

21264-5 Paperbound $3.00

ON THE LAWS OF JAPANESE PAINTING, H. P. Bowie. This classic work on the philosophy and technique of Japanese art is based on the author's first-hand experiences studying art in Japan. Every aspect of Japanese painting is described: the use of the brush and other materials; laws governing conception and execution; subjects for Japanese paintings, etc. The best possible substitute for a series of lessons from a great Oriental master. Index. xv + 117pp. + 66 plates. 6⅛ x 9¼.

20030-2 Paperbound $5.00

A HANDBOOK OF ANATOMY FOR ART STUDENTS, Arthur Thomson. This long-popular text teaches any student, regardless of level of technical competence, all the subtleties of human anatomy. Clear photographs, numerous line sketches and diagrams of bones, joints, etc. Use it as a text for home study, as a supplement to life class work, or as a lifelong sourcebook and reference volume. Author's prefaces. 67 plates, containing 40 line drawings, 86 photographs—mostly full page. 211 figures. Appendix. Index. xx + 459pp. 5⅜ x 8⅜. 21163-0 Paperbound $5.00

WHITTLING AND WOODCARVING, E. J. Tangerman. With this book, a beginner who is moderately handy can whittle or carve scores of useful objects, toys for children, gifts, or simply pass hours creatively and enjoyably. "Easy as well as instructive reading," N. Y. Herald Tribune Books. 464 illustrations, with appendix and index. x + 293pp. 5½ x 8⅛.

20965-2 Paperbound $3.50

ONE HUNDRED AND ONE PATCHWORK PATTERNS, Ruby Short McKim. Whether you have made a hundred quilts or none at all, you will find this the single most useful book on quiltmaking. There are 101 full patterns (all exact size) with full instructions for cutting and sewing. In addition there is some really choice folklore about the origin of the ingenious pattern names: "Monkey Wrench," "Road to California," "Drunkard's Path," "Crossed Canoes," to name a few. Over 500 illustrations. 124 pp. 7⅞ x 10¾. 20773-0 Paperbound $3.00

ART AND GEOMETRY, W. M. Ivins, Jr. Challenges the idea that the foundations of modern thought were laid in ancient Greece. Pitting Greek tactile-muscular intuitions of space against modern visual intuitions, the author, for 30 years curator of prints, Metropolitan Museum of Art, analyzes the differences between ancient and Renaissance painting and sculpture and tells of the first fruitful investigations of perspective. x + 113pp. 5⅜ x 8⅜. 20941-5 Paperbound $2.00

VITRUVIUS: TEN BOOKS ON ARCHITECTURE. The most influential book in the history of architecture. 1st century A.D. Roman classic has influenced such men as Bramante, Palladio, Michelangelo, up to present. Classic principles of design, harmony, etc. Fascinating reading. Definitive English translation by Professor H. Morgan, Harvard. 344pp. 5⅜ x 8.

20645-9 Paperbound $4.00

HAWTHORNE ON PAINTING. Vivid re-creation, from students' notes, of instructions by Charles Hawthorne at Cape Cod School of Art. Essays, epigrammatic comments on color, form, seeing, techniques, etc. "Excellent," Time. 100pp. 5⅜ x 8.

20653-X Paperbound $2.00

THE HANDBOOK OF PLANT AND FLORAL ORNAMENT, *R. G. Hatton.* 1200 line illustrations, from medieval, Renaissance herbals, of flowering or fruiting plants: garden flowers, wild flowers, medicinal plants, poisons, industrial plants, etc. A unique compilation that probably could not be matched in any library in the world. Formerly "The Craftsman's Plant-Book." Also full text on uses, history as ornament, etc. 548pp. 6⅛ x 9¼.

20649-1 Paperbound $6.00

DECORATIVE ALPHABETS AND INITIALS, *Alexander Nesbitt.* 91 complete alphabets, over 3900 ornamental initials, from Middle Ages, Renaissance printing, baroque, rococo, and modern sources. Individual items copyright free, for use in commercial art, crafts, design, packaging, etc. 123 full-page plates. 3924 initials. 129pp. 7¾ x 10¾.   20544-4 Paperbound $5.00

METHODS AND MATERIALS OF THE GREAT SCHOOLS AND MASTERS, *Sir Charles Eastlake.* (Formerly titled "Materials for a History of Oil Painting.") Vast, authentic reconstruction of secret techniques of the masters, recreated from ancient manuscripts, contemporary accounts, analysis of paintings, etc. Oils, fresco, tempera, varnishes, encaustics. Both Flemish and Italian schools, also British and French. One of great works for art historians, critics; inexhaustible mine of suggestions, information for practicing artists. Total of 1025pp. 5⅜ x 8.

20718-8, 20719-6 Two volume set, Paperbound $12.00

A HISTORY OF COSTUME, *Carl Köhler.* The most reliable and authentic account of the development of dress from ancient times through the 19th century. Based on actual pieces of clothing that have survived, using paintings, statues and other reproductions only where originals no longer exist. Hundreds of illustrations, including detailed patterns for many articles. Highly useful for theatre and movie directors, fashion designers, illustrators, teachers. Edited and augmented by Emma von Sichart. 594 illustrations. 464pp. 5⅛ x 7⅛.   21030-8   Paperbound $5.00

THE HUMAN FIGURE, *J. H. Vanderpoel.* Not just a picture book, but a complete course by a famous figure artist. Extensive text, illustrated by 430 pencil and charcoal drawings of both male and female anatomy. 2nd enlarged edition. Foreword. 430 illus. 143pp. 6⅛ x 9¼.   20432-4 Paperbound $2.50

GREEK REVIVAL ARCHITECTURE IN AMERICA, T. Hamlin. A comprehensive study of the American Classical Revival, its regional variations, reasons for its success and eventual decline. Profusely illustrated with photos, sketches, floor plans and sections, displaying the work of almost every important architect of the time. 2 appendices. 39 figures, 94 plates containing 221 photos, 62 architectural designs, drawings, etc. 324-item classified bibliography. Index. xi + 439pp. 5⅜ x 8½.

21148-7   Paperbound $5.00

CREATIVE LITHOGRAPHY AND HOW TO DO IT, Grant Arnold. Written by a man who practiced and taught lithography for many years, this highly useful volume explains all the steps of the lithographic process from tracing the drawings on the stone to printing the lithograph, with helpful hints for solving special problems. Index. 16 reproductions of lithographs. 11 drawings. xv + 214pp. of text. 5⅜ x 8½.

21208-4   Paperbound $3.50

THE STANDARD BOOK OF QUILT MAKING AND COLLECTING, M. Ickis. Even if you are a beginner, you will soon find yourself quilting like an expert, by following these clearly drawn patterns, photographs, and step-by-step instructions. Over 40 full-size patterns. Index. 483 illustrations. One color plate. xi + 276pp. 6¾ x 9½.   20582-7   Paperbound $3.50

PAINTING IN THE FAR EAST, L. Binyon. A study of over 1500 years of Oriental art by one of the world's outstanding authorities. The author chooses the most important masters in each period—Wu Tao-tzu, Toba Sojo, Kanaoka, Li Lung-mien, Masanobu, Okio, etc.—and examines the works, schools, and influence of each within their cultural context. 42 photographs. Sources of original works and selected bibliography. Notes including list of principal painters by periods. xx + 297pp. 6⅛ x 9¼.

20520-7   Paperbound $5.00

THE ALPHABET AND ELEMENTS OF LETTERING, F. W. Goudy. A beautifully illustrated volume on the aesthetics of letters and type faces and their history and development. Each plate consists of 15 forms of a single letter with the last plate devoted to the ampersand and the numerals. "A sound guide for all persons engaged in printing or drawing," Saturday Review. 27 full-page plates. 48 additional figures. xii + 131pp. 7⅞ x 10¾.

20792-7   Paperbound $3.50

THE COMPLETE BOOK OF SILK SCREEN PRINTING PRODUCTION, J. I. Biegeleisen. Here is a clear and complete picture of every aspect of silk screen technique and press operation—from individually operated manual presses to modern automatic ones. Unsurpassed as a guidebook for setting up shop, making shop operation more efficient, finding out about latest methods and equipment; or as a textbook for use in teaching, studying, or learning all aspects of the profession. 124 figures. Index. Bibliography. List of Supply Sources. xi + 253pp. 5⅜ x 8½.

21100-2   Paperbound $2.95

Dover Books on Art

PENNSYLVANIA DUTCH AMERICAN FOLK ART, H. J. Kauffman. The originality and charm of this early folk art give it a special appeal even today, and surviving pieces are sought by collectors all over the country. Here is a rewarding introductory guide to the Dutch country and its household art, concentrating on pictorial matter—hex signs, tulip ware, weather vanes, interiors, paintings and folk sculpture, rocking horses and children's toys, utensils, Stiegel-type glassware, etc. "A serious, worthy and helpful volume," W. G. Dooley, N. Y. TIMES. Introduction. Bibliography. 279 halftone illustrations. 28 motifs and other line drawings. 1 map. 146pp. 7⅞ x 10¾.

21205-X Paperbound $4.00

DESIGN AND EXPRESSION IN THE VISUAL ARTS, J. F. A. Taylor. Here is a much needed discussion of art theory which relates the new and sometimes bewildering directions of 20th century art to the great traditions of the past. The first discussion of principle that addresses itself to the eye rather than to the intellect, using illustrations from Rembrandt, Leonardo, Mondrian, El Greco, etc. List of plates. Index. 59 reproductions. 5 color plates. 75 figures. x + 245pp. 5⅜ x 8½.

21195-9 Paperbound $3.50

THE ENJOYMENT AND USE OF COLOR, W. Sargent. Requiring no special technical know-how, this book tells you all about color and how it is created, perceived, and imitated in art. Covers many little-known facts about color values, intensities, effects of high and low illumination, complementary colors, and color harmonies. Simple do-it-yourself experiments and observations. 35 illustrations, including 6 full-page color plates. New color frontispiece. Index. x + 274 pp. 5⅜ x 8.

20944-X Paperbound $3.50

STYLES IN PAINTING, Paul Zucker. By comparing paintings of similar subject matter, the author shows the characteristics of various painting styles. You are shown at a glance the differences between reclining nudes by Giorgione, Velasquez, Goya, Modigliani; how a Byzantine portrait is unlike a portrait by Van Eyck, da Vinci, Dürer, or Marc Chagall; how the painting of landscapes has changed gradually from ancient Pompeii to Lyonel Feininger in our own century. 241 beautiful, sharp photographs illustrate the text. xiv + 338 pp. 5⅝ x 8¼.

20760-9 Paperbound $4.00

Dover publishes books on commercial art, art history, crafts, design, art classics; also books on music, literature, science, mathematics, puzzles and entertainments, chess, engineering, biology, philosophy, psychology, languages, history, and other fields. For free circulars write to Dept. DA, Dover Publications, Inc., 180 Varick St., New York, N.Y. 10014.